First published 2001 by Silvio Mattacchione & Co.
1251 Scugog Line 8, RR#1.
Port Perry, ON, Canada L9L 1B2
Telephone: 905.985.3555
Fax: 905.985.4005
www.silvio-co.com

National Library of Canada Cataloguing in Publication Data

Borner, Tessa
Potholes to Paradise

ISBN 1-895270-21-9

1. New business enterprises - Costa Rica. I. Title

HD62.5.B675 2001   658.1'1'097286   C2001-930101-4

Design and Production
*Silvio Mattacchione and Co.
Studio Graziano and Associates Inc.
pgraziano@sympatico.ca*

*Printed and bound in Canada
by Friesens, Manitoba*

Potholes to Paradise

BY TESSA BORNER

3

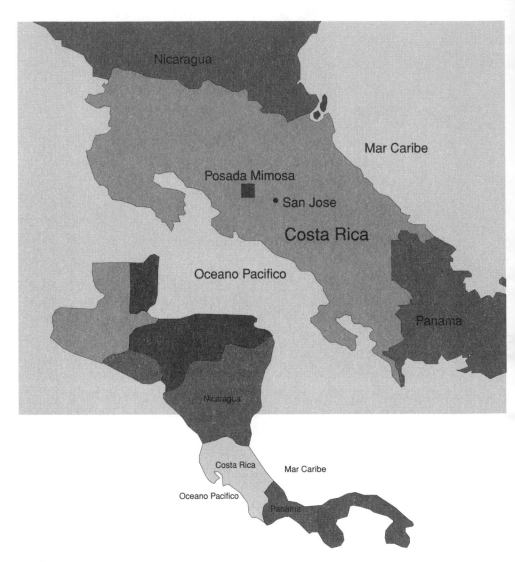

4

This book
is dedicated
to all those
courageous
souls
who dare
to follow their
dreams!

5

Acknowledgements

The challenge in writing this book has been keeping abreast of the unprecedented changes in Costa Rican life and culture since we first came here in 1987. My thanks and gratitude go first of all to my husband and co-adventurer Martin for his patient support and critical eye. Many thanks to my daughter Megan Borner Jourdain for introducing me to her colleague Janice Dyer who pulled the book together with her fine editing skills. Where would I have been without Paul Jourdain's daunting computer skills?

Tessa and Martin

Thanks also to the people I interviewed for contributing their insights and experiences in Costa Rica. In some cases names have been changed to protect their privacy.

Every effort has been made to ensure this book is as up-to-date as possible. With the frequent changes in laws, telephone numbers, prices and travel information, it is quite likely some information is liable to change.

Tessa Borner

6

Table of Contents

Chapter 3:
Travelling to Costa Rica

Chapter 4:
Getting To and Getting Around Costa Rica

Chapter 5:
Where To Go and What To See

9

Chapter 6:
Health Care

Chapter 7:
How to Obtain Residency

Chapter 8:
Setting Up a Business

Chapter 9:
All About Real Estate

Chapter 10:
Running a Bed and Breakfast

Chapter 11:
Costa Rica Diary and Updates

Chapter 12:
Updates After the Move

Chapter 13:
Epilogue

Appendices

Foreword

If you like to do your own thing, dislike large tour groups, genuinely love and appreciate variety of scenery, nature and animal life, enjoy a warm climate, like adventure sports, are a rugged individualist, are patient and not easily frustrated, like friendly service, appreciate the qualities of gentle, patient people (except when behind the wheel of a car!), enjoy being able to walk the streets without fear (except some areas of San Jose), then Costa Rica is for you.

Never mind what pre-conceived idea you may have of Costa Rica being a "cheap" destination – for tourists, it is not. If you are coming from a Florida mind-set, forget it. If you think you will find long, never-ending stretches of white sandy beaches as in the southern United States or Hawaii, forget it. If you are unable to deal with the unexpected or get easily irritated when your best-laid plans do not work out, Costa Rica is not for you. If you like manicured lawns, community living with people like you, and pulsating nightlife, it's not for you. If you are a golf nut, there are only a few decent 18-hole courses (although more have sprung up in the last couple of years). Keep in mind that Costa Rica is a Third World country, albeit a highly civilized one.

In 1993, I started writing a series of newsletters "Around and About Costa Rica" in response to the difficulty we had in getting answers to our questions about Costa

From the Posada Mimosa guest book:

We are both so pleased that we saw your sign from the road. It is our second trip to Costa Rica and the last night of our current adventure. Your home, gardens and view are magnificent. We are so happy to have a soft bed and face cloths. As I have read in this guest book you have provided both comfort and "paradise" to several Canadians... add us to the list... We will spread the news.

Owen & Wendy, Calgary, Alberta

Rica. At that time there were few guidebooks and little other information.

I continued writing them until April 1995, when the pressure of moving and adjusting to another culture, as well as starting a Bed & Breakfast, took all of my time. I decided to update them and put them in book form for the benefit of North Americans and others who are thinking of moving here. I want to try and bring the Costa Rican experience into perspective by sharing my family's personal story, and that of other people who have adopted this country as their own. Using our own continuing story as a model, I will give you practical tips on traveling, running a business and retiring in Costa Rica, as well as unravelling some of its cultural peculiarities.

Having lived here for six years, we have discovered two faces of Costa Rica – the light, bright, smiling and open demeanour and the enigmatic, closed and darker side hidden below a passive surface. In the last three years, Costa's Rica's pristine image has been tarnished by a rise in crime, which often happens when tourism grows as quickly as it has here. The travelling public needs to know that this is a country like any other, with its share of good and bad. It is not simply "paradise."

Until now, Costa Rica has relied on its natural beauty and innocence to succeed as a travel destination. Now that is not enough. It is time to face reality and acknowledge Costa Rica has its share of problems, as all countries do. Costa Rica can no longer solely rely on its peaceful image and unique eco-tourism now that there is peace throughout Central America and other countries in the region can offer similar attractions.

14

To give a balanced view of Costa Rica, I interviewed people who have made their homes here. I have included excerpts from these interviews in the shaded boxes in the text so that you may experience a range of perspectives.

My goal is to present a realistic impression so that you can make an informed decision and hopefully avoid some of the "potholes to paradise."

NOTE:

The following pages may seem somewhat negative or even alarming at first. I do not believe in "pussyfooting" or looking through rose-coloured glasses. So if I shock the reader and help you to come down to earth, you will be better served in the long run.

In spite of all the trials and tribulations, we are glad we are here. When we travel away, we cannot wait to get back. *As you read on, you will see that we have experienced many "magic moments."*

Chapter 1
Why Costa Rica?

Our First Visit

My husband Martin and I first visited Costa Rica in 1987. We were looking for a new and interesting holiday destination, free of inhospitable natives, cold commercialism and mundane tour packages. It was Christmas time, and yes, we did make that first visit with *Fiesta Holidays!* We spent a delightful two weeks and vowed to return some day. Little did we know that 13 years

later we would be living and running a business here, and that our youngest son would be doing the same!

From 1990 to 1993, we travelled to Europe and other warm climates in search of the ideal place to live and eventually retire. We ruled out Europe because of escalating political and social problems, and the southern United States because of rising crime and high medical and insurance costs. We have never been fans of the Caribbean, feeling that island living can become claustrophobic after awhile. We considered Mexico, but were concerned about poor sanitation.

Costa Rica came closest to meeting our criteria for what we thought would be a relatively trouble-free life:

- accessible and available health care;
- moderate climate;
- reasonable tax rate;
- available and affordable household help;
- total lifestyle change.

Tourism

Since 1993, tourism in Costa Rica has changed dramatically. Tourism overtook coffee as Costa Rica's biggest foreign revenue earner in 1993 by growing at a phenomenal rate of just under 20 percent per year between 1990 and 1993. By the 1994-1995 season, the growth rate had slowed down substantially. In 1996, tourism declined, and the number of tourists flying into Juan Santa Maria airport fell by 4.2 percent.

According to statistics compiled by the Costa Rican Tourism Office (ICT), the number of international tourist arrivals at Juan Santa Maria Airport increased by 12.2% from May 1997-May 1998. The number of North American visitors increased by 24.9% while visitors from Europe showed a small increase of 1%, with a decrease in the number of visitors from Germany, England and Italy. From January to May 1998, the number of visitors from the United States increased by 24.4%. Similarly, Canadian visitors increased by 18.4%, although a spokesperson at the Canadian Embassy questioned the accuracy of these statistics because they include all arrivals, not just tourists (e.g., business people, foreign residents, etc.). The total number of tourists in 1999 was 1,021,138, up from 781,127 in 1996.

The ICT statistics for the first three months of 2000 showed strong growth in the number of tourists from the Northern countries of Europe. The number of tourists arriving in the first trimester of 2000 compared to the same period in 1999 rose by 19.6% from Germany, 13% from Austria, 31.6% from Holland and 17.2% from Switzerland. Last year, 46% of tourists to Costa Rica were from Canada, the United States and Mexico, while only 14% were from Europe.

With the advent of tourism has come a rise in crime, previously unheard of in this country. Crime used to be restricted to non-violent petty thievery. Now we have had kidnappings, attacks on tourists and armed robberies, which have tainted Costa Rica's hitherto pristine image. Nevertheless, in comparison to the United States and other western countries, crime is still on a small scale. Unfortunately, one or two isolated incidents have been blown way out of proportion. Recently, the government has placed tourist police in the most popular spots to help reduce incidents.

According to a spokesperson at the Canadian Embassy, Costa Rica is doing more and more promotion abroad, but says little about the potential problems facing tourists. The government has done little to improve the country's infrastructure, curb over-pricing, post warning signs in dangerous areas (e.g., beaches where there are strong rip-tides), or car rental problems.

John and Mary:

"I think that a lot of the things we were led to believe Costa Rica was, is not true, definitely not true. The country is beautiful but a lot of the information we had before we moved here turned out to be wrong. I think living here is fine, doing business is another story. We have an American friend who lives here, has his money and business in another country. He says that's the perfect combination."

The worst and most persistent crime of all is "business" crime. The trust factor is a fleeting one – some expatriate North Americans defraud, embezzle and engage in all manner of dishonest practices with fellow expatriates. We know of several people who, like ourselves, have

18

been relieved of their money by unscrupulous scam-artists. There are also Costa Ricans with whom we have dealt in business who are equally guilty. It is a problem that nobody seems to address and with which the justice system deals very slowly or not at all. There are ways to protect yourself, however, and I hope to help you avoid some of these problems.

About Us

"We" are a couple enjoying "non retirement" in Costa Rica and experiencing a total change in lifestyle! Martin, originally from Germany, is an international commercial, industrial and investment real estate broker. I am originally from England, and I am a journalist and teacher of English as a Second or Foreign Language. We lived in Canada for many years, where two of our children and seven of our grandchildren still live.

Our eldest daughter recently remarried and moved to New Zealand with her four children.

Jason, 30, the youngest of our five children, settled in Costa Rica and created "Ecotreks Adventure Company." He specializes in sailing charters aboard his 36-foot Columbia for individuals and groups. He also sponsors mountain biking races, and has spearheaded beach clean-ups and other ecological projects. After living at Flamingo Beach for six years, he has relocated to the Osa Peninsula where he continues to do sailing charters, research whales and dolphins and has started a turtle hatchery to protect them from poaching and to help in the survival of this endangered species.

> To contact ECOTREKS, tel/fax: (506) 494-5868;
> e-mail: tervoz@racsa.co.cr

"Posada Mimosa"

We officially opened our Bed and Breakfast, "Posada Mimosa," in December 1996 and since then have received a steady flow of guests. We have been described as one of the best B & B's in the Central Valley. We are proud to say that "Posada Mimosa" has been awarded two stars and is listed in the New Key to Costa Rica under "Lodgings Practicing Sustainable Tourism."

Lodging "sustainability" is defined as having a low impact on the environment, supporting the local economy, and promoting the best of local culture. Lodgings are classified according to one, two or three star ratings. Our two star rating was based on the following:

(1) we grow plants which attract birds & butterflies;

(2) Martin works on various conservation projects in Grecia and is marketing a product for organic agriculture;

(3) we use solar heating to conserve energy;

(4) we use biodegradable products;

(5) we have installed "lo-flo"showers;

(6) our buildings are architecturally designed to conserve energy;

(7) we provide tourist information;

(8) we encourage tourists to support local restaurants, shops, etc.

(9) we hire local employees;

(10) we help the local community;

(11) we have learned a lot in a short time about Costa Rica;

(12) we have respect for and integrate with the local culture.

Why Costa Rica?

Why did we choose Costa Rica? Perhaps the most dramatic reason was an emergency triple by-pass Martin underwent here on one of our first visits! Our experience with the superb private medical care in Costa Rica made good available health care a number one priority. The next reason was the climate – we no longer wanted to put up with sub-zero temperatures, sunless days, wearing heavy clothes and slipping and sliding on snow-laden roads during Canadian winters. There are few places in the world that enjoy the wonderful weather of Grecia and its surroundings. The third reason was the high taxes we were paying in Canada. The availability of household help is another big plus to this country because, if we get sick and as we get older, we will be well looked after by caring Costa Ricans.

The biggest reason for choosing Costa Rica was that we wanted a complete change of lifestyle with new and interesting challenges. Running a Bed and Breakfast was something I had always wanted to do. We are happy to say we have achieved that goal very successfully, although as you will see, the path was not always easy and was fraught with obstacles.

For Martin, the change of lifestyle was a necessity. The day after the by-pass operation, the Costa Rican surgeon told him that the operation went well and, if he lives a less stressful life, he can probably count on 15 more years. That was good news. The day before surgery, his life expectancy was less than a week. Nevertheless, the reality of this statement was shocking: it made him think of his real priorities for the time he has left. Nobody knows whether it is 15, 12 or 22 years, but the finality of it hits hard. So if that's all there is, what is a worthwhile course to take?

The "old" business of real estate investments was out – much too stressful. What really counts for Martin is the well-being of our grandchildren, who deserve a healthy environment. So environment it is: clean air, water and agriculture free of chemicals. Costa Rica has 365 growing days and a different climate with every 100 metres change of elevation, making it an ideal place to work and experiment.

Six years later, Martin is importing organic Penac products from Germany. He has helped the largest tomato farmer in the Central Valley to increase his crop by 50% and decrease the need for chemicals by 70%. He has eliminated the tomato leaf blight (of Irish potato famine fame). He has achieved similar results with strawberries, other vegetables, fruit trees and coffee. Instead of burning the sugar cane fields, he used Penac to stimulate the composting of the leaves on the ground and improve the organic matter in the soil. It resulted in a 98% yield the next harvest.

At one point in his work, Martin needed some soil with nematodes (microscopic bugs that attack the roots of many plants). They are killed with horrible nematocides that destroy everything in the soil (then we eat the fruit). They return six months later and more poison is sprayed. He went to a coffee plantation on the slopes of the Poas Volcano and asked the farmer if he could please have some nematodes. The farmer replied "Sure, you can have them all!" Next thing he knew, Martin was lying on his stomach under the coffee bushes, with a spoon and a plastic bag, digging for a soil sample. As he looked underneath the bushes, he could see the whole farm. He started to laugh, and thought "am I crazy?" The real estate executive who made multi-million dollar deals, lying on his stomach digging for nematodes! Then he looked up through the lush green leaves into the dark blue sky and said: "but I love it!" So if you feel a change of lifestyle is for you – Costa Rica may be it!

Anyone concerned about the environment should read From Naked Ape to Super Species by David Suzuki and Holly Dressel.

Costa Rica is an interesting place to be with many things to do. We have made good friends who are involved in diverse and fascinating projects. Anything is possible here, but you need great "stickability" and tremendous patience! It goes without saying that living in spectacular surroundings, in harmony with nature, and among warm, friendly people, is not too difficult to take!

Rick and Marge **moved to Costa Rica and opened a butterfly and insect collection:**

"Costa Ricans in general are wonderful people, happy, "pura vida" is the most common expression you hear. They love music, particularly classical music. The country is absolutely indescribable - a paradise - I can't possibly imagine going back to live in North America. Here it's like springtime every day. It cannot be described to a person who has not been here they have to experience it themselves. It is hard to leave your country, change your language, leave your family, particularly if you have had some kind of steady job or business, to suddenly be without that."

Who Chooses to Live in Costa Rica?

There are six categories of foreigners who choose to live in Costa Rica:

(1) retirees;

(2) business people transferred by their companies;

(3) entrepreneurs;

(4) people devoted to nature and ecology;

(5) fugitives and losers;

(6) old-timers.

Generally speaking, categories (1) and (2) continue living the way they have lived anywhere else. They live in gated communities with like-minded people, some resist learning Spanish, and they join Gringo clubs and chew the fat in Gringo bars. Nothing much has changed for them except the climate and maybe the cost of living.

Category (3) includes the people who come to Costa Rica independently, with energy, initiative and enthusiasm, and contribute greatly to the economy in a wide variety of enterprises. I am constantly amazed at the range of ages of people who move here – 5 years old to 80, young families as well as retirees!

Category (4) includes people who sincerely want to improve the environment, preserve the natural beauty of this diverse country and help local communities. They initiate and develop interesting and varied ecological projects. Also included in this category are church groups who generously contribute their time to building projects and job creation.

Category (5) includes the low-life in any society. Fugitives are generally running away from something or somebody and spend their time preying on the unsuspecting, fabricating unscrupulous deals in any way they can. Unfortunately, Costa Rica seems to have more than its fair share of these individuals. Losers are generally people running away from themselves and think they will finally "find" themselves in Costa Rica, but often end up living on the beach in an alcoholic stupor.

Category (6), old-timers, are people who have lived here at least ten years or longer and are fully integrated into Costa Rican life.

John and Mary moved to Costa Rica with their 3 children in 1994, and have found the transition difficult:

We had lunch with some people from Canada last week and the gentleman made a comment which I think was very good. Most of the people he has met in the four years he has been living in Costa Rica have reinvented themselves into somebody else! People who come down here to start businesses they know absolutely nothing about – they are reinventing themselves! We have met a lot of flakes here. When you look at all the foreigners living here, there are not a lot of people with any kind of substance to them. They're drifters, they couldn't make it there and they think they can make it here. In fact when our kids went to school after we first arrived here, the other kids said to them "so what are your parents running away from?"

Chapter 2
Costa Rica at a Glance

The following information was compiled from the Internet, interviews and our personal experiences.

Location

Central America, bordering both the Caribbean Sea and the North Pacific Ocean, between Nicaragua and Panama.

Size

Total area: 51,100 sq km (slightly smaller than West Virginia).

Coastline: 1,290 km.

Length North to South: 440 km.

Driving time coast-to-coast: About five hours (more like seven in reality due to the road conditions!)

Highest point: Mt. Chirripo – 3,810 meters.

Electrical Current

110 V

Major Cities

San Jose, Alajuela, Cartago, Puntarenas, Limon, Heredia, Liberia.

Time Zone

Central Standard (GMT minus 6 hours) – same time as Winnipeg, Chicago and Dallas.

Climate

Tropical: dry season (December to April); rainy season (May to November).

Temperatures: Vary from steamy tropical heat (over 90F) in the lowlands to near-freezing in the high mountains, with a year-round average in the Central Valley of 72F (22C), depending on where you live. (For example, Grecia and Atenas are much warmer than San Jose and Escazu, and enjoy more sunshine and less rain). Costa Rica has many micro climates, check them out before settling somewhere.

Population

3,604,642 (July 1998 est.)

Ethnic groups: white (including mestizo) – 96%; black – 2%; Indian – 1%; Chinese – 1%.

Religion: Primarily Roman Catholic (95%).

Languages: Spanish (official language); English is spoken on the Caribbean coast where descendants of Jamaican immigrants live.

Literacy rate: 93%, higher than the United States and Canada. Many of the poor cannot afford to go to school because of the high cost of uniforms and books. The public school system is very traditional. New bilingual schools with more progressive methods are springing up all the time.

Government

Independent democratic republic – Latin America's oldest democracy.

Independence: September 15, 1821 (from Spain).

National Holidays

Independence Day, September 15.

Other important holidays include Christmas, Semana Santa (Holy Week & Easter) and the month of July, when San Jose empties and everyone heads for the beaches (Playa Coco and Playa Nosara are favourites).

There are at least eight other minor holidays throughout the year.

Economy

Costa Rica's basically stable and progressive economy depends especially on tourism and the export of bananas, coffee and other agricultural products. Poverty has been substantially reduced over the past 15 years, and a strong social safety net has been put in place. Recent trends, however, have been disappointing. Economic growth slipped from 4.3% in 1994 to 2.5% in 1995, to 0.9% in 1996, and then rebounded in 1997 to 3%. Inflation has been unstable over the last few years: 13.5% in 1994, 22.5% in 1995, 17.5% in 1996, 11.2% in 1997, 12.3% in 1998 and 10.11% in 1999.

Unemployment appears moderate at 5.7%, but substantial underemployment continues. Furthermore, large government deficits have undermined efforts to maintain the quality of social services.

The government faces a formidable task to curb inflation, reduce the deficit, encourage domestic savings, and do all this in harmony with International Monetary Fund agreements. One important positive development – the infusion of more than $200 million in 1997 by microchip giant Intel and the anticipated attraction of other high-tech firms to Costa Rica will help stimulate growth and employment over the next several years.

GDP purchasing power parity: $19.6 billion (1997)

GDP real growth rate: 3%(1997 est.)

GDP per capita, purchasing power parity: $5,500 (1997 est.)

GDP composition by sector: agriculture 18%; industry 24%; services 58%(1995)

Exports: $3.82 billion (1996)

Commodities: coffee, bananas, textiles, sugar

Main partners: United States, Germany, Italy, Guatemala, El Salvador, Netherlands, United Kingdom, France.

Imports: $3.85 (1996)

Commodities: raw materials, consumer goods, capital equipment, petroleum

Main partners: United States, Japan, Mexico, Guatemala, Venezuela, Germany

Industries: Food processing, textiles and clothing, construction materials, fertilizer, plastic products.

Agriculture: Accounts for 19% of GDP and 70% of exports; cash commodities – coffee, beef, bananas, sugar; other food crops include corn, rice, beans, potatoes; normally self-sufficient in food except for grain; depletion of forest resources resulting in lower timber output.

30

Expatriates

Expatriates number at least 25,000 and there could be as many as 40,000 from different countries. Most live in the central valley, but a fair number are scattered throughout the country. The *Associacion de Residentes* (formerly *Association of Pensionados-Rentistas of Costa Rica*) looks after the interests of expatriates and provides numerous services for members at reasonable costs. These services include speedy mail service outside the country, counselling and processing paperwork for residency, referring people to real estate agents, providing private group medical insurance with no age limit, processing drivers licenses and generally guiding new arrivals through the bureaucratic minefield.

Annual dues are $50 US for residents, $100 US for tourists, and $10 US for each additional dependent. They also have social gatherings and seminars to provide information about living in Costa Rica. The Association now has 800 members.

Contact: Apdo. 1191-1007, Centro Colon, San Jose, Costa Rica; tel: 011-506-233-1017; 221-2053, 257-6646; fax: 011-506-222-78-62. E-mail: arcrsacc@sol.racsa.co.cr website: http//www.casacanada.net/arcr

Business Hours

Banks: 9 a.m. to 3 p.m.

Government offices: 8 a.m. to 5 p.m.

Shops and shopping centres: 9 a.m. to 7 p.m.

There is a two-hour lunch break. Some of the larger shopping centres are open on Sundays.

Average Salary
$250-300 US a month.

Telephone Numbers
To phone from North America – 011-506 plus the number.

To phone in Costa Rica – AT & T: 114

International Operator – 116

International; Information – 124

Canada Direct – 0800-015-1161 (using Bell calling card)

USA Direct – 0800-012-2222 (mci)

AT & T Operator – 0800-11-4114

Telephone numbers for Costa Rican Consulates in Canada:

Ottawa: 613-562-2855 or 613-562-2956

Vancouver: 604-681-2152

Montreal: 514-393-1057

Toronto: 416-961-6773

Health Care
Although Costa Rica is considered the Third World (in 1996 it was elevated to Second World status by the US), the grinding, visible poverty and begging that is so prevalent in Mexico and other Latin American countries is less evident here. Instead, one is impressed by the seemingly high education and health standards enjoyed by the whole population, be they rich or poor.

In reality, there are two health standards – private clinics for those who can afford it, and the deteriorating public system. People must line up at three or four o'clock in the morning to get an appointment with a doctor. They can wait as long as a year to receive cortisone injections, for example, which are over-used here for almost any ache or pain.

Our maid's mother suffered a stroke and went to the Hospital de Mexico in San Jose, but was sent back home because she was not on the public insurance and could not pay. Once at home, she called a doctor who also refused to attend to her for the same reasons. The lesson is: no insurance, no money, no health care. The public system is over-burdened with accident and sickness claims. In 1995 alone, there were 600,000 claims with billions of colones paid out and this for a population of just 3.5 million.

Environmental Issues

Current issues include deforestation, largely a result of the clearing of land for cattle ranching and soil erosion. Natural hazards include occasional earthquakes, hurricanes along the Atlantic coast, frequent flooding of lowlands at the onset of the rainy season, and active volcanoes.

The public image of Costa Rica is of a country concerned about preserving its rain forests, animal and bird life and its environment. Yet, outside the jungles, especially in San Jose, pollution clogs the lungs and stings the eyes. Garbage is thrown in the streets, although there is now a law fining people who litter. Like most laws here, it is probably rarely enforced. Smoke belches uncontrolled out of trucks, buses and cars which should never be allowed on the roads; raw sewage still pollutes rivers and oceans; burgeoning construction is everywhere and one wonders who is going to win the battle of the environment - the environmentalists or big business.

Since 1996, motor vehicles have to pass a strict inspection to earn an "eco-marchamo," a sticker that goes on the windshield to show that the vehicle meets environmental standards. Without the "eco-marchamo", a vehicle will not be issued a regular "marchamo" which is another sticker that goes on the windshield. It is another way of earning more tax money and ensuring that smoke-belching vehicles will be banned from the roads, although progress is slow and pollution is still a major problem. The next step is to work on noise pollution and ban trucks from the roads whose noise level is deafening, and stop night flights that shatter a peaceful night's sleep in the Central Valley.

When President Figueres came to power in 1994, there were signs of progress. His government brought in stiff fines for farmers who pollute rivers with coffee wastes or burn the sugar cane. In reality, farmers are still burning their cane, destroying wildlife, polluting the air and raining cinders and ash everywhere. We have heard that farmers actually get permits to burn their cane even though it is against the law!

However, it is not all bad. In Grecia, we have a very good environmental group who successfully closed down the garbage dump that smouldered night and day. It produced a constant black smoke hanging over the valley causing health problems such as asthma. This was one small victory by citizens who would not put up with it any more.

34

Rick and Marge:

As I speak, every second, an area of rain forest the size of a football field and all the animals and plants there are destroyed day and night. In Brazil, there is not only the rainy season and the dry season but also the burning season when rain forest fires are so enormous and cover such huge areas they are visible from space. Even if we do a tiny amount to save them, it is at least something and it is better than sitting up North watching CNN and being told about the destruction of the rain forests.

A glaring example of flagrant disregard for the environment is a mega resort on the beach with hundreds of rooms and all the ugly trappings of mass tourism. In the past, there were protests and boycotts against the hotel. The Spanish group allegedly violated many environmental protection laws during its construction. They denuded the land of trees, allegedly destroying mangroves and violating health laws. They also changed the course of rivers and built within the 50-metre mark of high tide. They treated workers poorly and did not obtain the required permits for construction and dynamiting, and two workers died in the process. In Costa Rica there is no follow-through on projects that are supposed to abide by the environmental laws: the government does not have the personnel to deal with it.

Protest groups persuaded scores of Spanish and German tour groups to boycott the hotel. What is more, in spite of the millions Costa Rica has spent on phone lines, power lines and roads for the project, most of the money earned goes right back to Spain where guests prepay. As well, the hotel is partially exempt from Costa Rican taxes for six years, thanks to government incentives for coastal development. The danger is that more resorts like this could be built in Costa Rica if greed wins out over idealism. Fortunately, there are moves afoot to prevent another similar situation.

Rick and Marge

When people come to our museum, it's not just a bunch of insects on the wall, it's artistically arranged butterflies with artificial plants in natural settings and the whole ambiance accented with classical music playing. We are personally involved with people and treat them like family and friends and they go away feeling like this is someone's home. Our main interest has not been economic but to teach people about the diminishing rain forest and the importance of Costa Rica in the world. Its unique location as a bottleneck between North and South America where millions of species have biodiversified due to the tremendous variety of plants that live here. Animals come from both North and South America and, as they come to Costa Rica, it is like a funnel where all these remarkable species come together in a unique blend that is not possible anywhere else on earth. Not only that, you have the changes in elevation in this little bottleneck, so you have animals and plants that can live in high mountains or in the hottest, most humid rain forest all squeezed into this small area. So if you are a biologist, it is absolute paradise.

A Short History

Christopher Columbus gave Costa Rica its name meaning "Rich Coast." On his fourth visit to the New World, he was inspired by Indians wearing a profusion of gold jewellery, and assumed he had stumbled upon a country rich with gold. Costa Rica was colonized more slowly than the rest of Central America. The Spanish could not build up a slave society because there were very few Indians, so the colonists had to do their own work. This lack of a slave culture is probably one of the main reasons why Costa

Rica could build a strong democracy. In 1821, Central America gained its independence from Spain but, at that time, Costa Rica was very poor and underdeveloped.

In the 19th century, the country began to export coffee and economic conditions improved. Attracting mostly German and Spanish immigrants, it became a more developed and cosmopolitan society. Descendants of those immigrants are the largest landowners today. The families who bought the largest chunks of land were the Peters who own all of Sarchi; Orlich (a former president) with land holdings in San Ramon; and Niehaus in Grecia who founded what is now Cooperativa Victoria (a very large farmers' co-operative processing plant for sugar cane and coffee). Other early settlers include the Sanchez-Arias who own most of Heredia (Oscar Arias is a Nobel Peace Prize winner), Oduber, Federspiel of Heredia, Kopper and Herrero. The Habsburgs of the Austrian-Hungarian Empire also bought thousands of acres in Guanacaste over one hundred years ago. A few British, Italians and others followed, but they did not acquire the land or wealth of these early arrivals.

At first, coffee was shipped out of the port of Puntarenas on the Pacific coast but eventually there was a need for an Atlantic port. Minor Keith, an American, built a railway through the jungle to the Caribbean town of Limon. It took 19 years to build and 400 workers died in the process. Jamaican, Italian and Chinese labourers helped build the railway and eventually settled in Costa Rica. The Caribbean coast is predominantly black and most of the descendants of Jamaicans still speak English. Minor Keith was given 800,000 acres in the Atlantic lowlands where he planted bananas, marking the beginning of his United Fruit Company, an important economic force in Central America for the next century.

Democracy came to Costa Rica in 1889 and has prevailed ever since, except for a couple of minor skirmishes – a 1917 military coup that lasted 30 months and a 1948 revolution that gave birth to the modern Costa Rica. Dr. Rafael Angel Calderon Guardia was one of the country's great social reformers, however he seized power through the army when his candidate lost an election in 1948.

A revolution followed, led by Jose "Pepe" Figueres, the father of the most recent past president. He sent Calderon into exile and drafted a new constitution, which abolished the army, but upheld most of Calderon's impressive social reforms. As a result, most of the money that other countries put into military defence goes into compulsory education, socialized medicine, a social security system and labour rights in Costa Rica. Oscar Arias, one of the country's past presidents, worked tirelessly to solve many of Central America's conflicts and won the Nobel Peace Prize in 1987.

Costa Rican society has been stable and healthy, free from the social turmoil that has marked the rest of Central America. In fact, many Costa Ricans consider themselves superior to the rest of Central America. However, this attitude is changing as the gap between the "haves" and "have-nots" widens, and Costa Ricans' frustrations increase with a government that does not listen to their concerns. One senses a powerlessness that is turning into militant action as the population is prepared to take matters into their own hands (e.g., the barricading of the town of Santa Ana in 1998 to protest the decision of the government to place the main garbage dump on its doorstep). Similar protests have also broken out in Limon, with an ever-increasing level of violence.

In the 1998 elections for a new president, the Social Christian Unity Party, led by Miguel Angel Rodriguez, ousted Figueres' National Liberation Party. He squeaked through by a margin of just 2 percent over his rival Jose Miguel Corrales. Twenty-nine percent of the population abstained from voting, indicating the growing cynicism.

Today, tourism has replaced coffee and bananas as Costa Rica's new source of income, due to the low prices coffee and bananas fetch in more competitive international markets. It is only in the last seven years that the tourism industry has increased so dramatically to become Costa Rica's number one industry.

The People and the Culture

The People

Costa Ricans are called "Ticos" and females are "Ticas". They are friendly and helpful, neat and invariably well dressed, especially when going shopping on Saturdays and on Sundays when families get together and eat out. Rarely does one see a child misbehaving and just as rarely does one see them being disciplined. Costa Ricans are not exuberantly "Latino" like their Mexican neighbours, but are rather more European and reserved. A Swiss couple we met observed that they had been trying to find that Latino spirit during their whole trip and had not found it. Perhaps they could understand why Costa Rica is called the Switzerland of Central America due to not only the scenery but also the personality of the people.

One does not find the extremes of rich and poor in Costa Rica. There is a predominantly educated middle class not often found in the rest of Latin America. Having said that, old wealth and ownership of huge hectares of land are still in the hands of a few families.

There are more than three million Ticos and about half of them live in the Central Valley in and around San Jose. They are predominantly of Spanish descent with fair complexions and refined, delicate features. One does not find as much of an indigenous mix as in other Latin-American countries because less than one percent of the population is full-blooded Indian, who mostly live in reservations around the *Talamanca Mountains*.

The Caribbean region has a large percentage of blacks along the coast, descendants of Jamaicans who came to work on the railroad. For a long time they were forbidden to live in the Central Valley, but that has now changed. A very subtle form of racism exists here: the whiter the skin, the better. When a baby is born, the greatest compliment you can give the mother is to say "Que blanco, Que gordo!" – "How white, how fat he is!"

The Chinese minority is spread evenly around the country and is mostly in the restaurant business. A large international community is centred mainly in the Central Valley. Europeans, mostly Spanish and Germans, have been in Costa Rica for over a 100 years and the first ones owned coffee plantations. Apparently they were on their way to the California Gold Rush in mid-1800 and stopped in Costa Rica, never to leave.

There is a large expatriate American community, many of whom first came to Costa Rica with the US Peace Corps and never returned to the States. There are also many American Legion members who spend their time reminiscing about various war exploits and are probably even more patriotic here than in the US! Canadian residents number about 1,200 families according to the Canadian Embassy. It is difficult to establish an accurate number because there are many Canadians who do not register with the Embassy. There are quite a few English-speaking schools and five universities in and around San Jose.

John and Mary

When we came here we put our children into a private American school that is fairly expensive - $5,000USD per year per child. They adapted very well to the small class size and the individual attention. The competition here is in academics not who has the nicest designer clothes. Here they have to wear uniforms, everybody is the same. So academic marks set them apart. The discipline is tenfold what it is in Canada. They do not take any nonsense. The kids are on a disciplinary notice system, where if they get three notices in the year, they are expelled and the fees are not refunded. The disciplinary notice is very strict – you can get it for not tucking your shirt in, for not doing your homework, for being late or missing school. Our girls have done very well and their Spanish is excellent.

The Culture

When we first came here, we naively thought that honesty prevailed. But we soon found out that, in a subtle sort of way, Ticos are very adept at extracting money. If they are going to do a job, for example in construction, they always want a lot of money up front. We no longer subscribe to this practice, having been burned once too often! They frequently expect to be paid before a job has been completed. They also hate confrontation, and we soon learned that

41

being impatient and aggressive achieves nothing. We have also found that lawyers carry a lot of weight, and threatening legal action does bring results. But beware of dishonest lawyers. Find out through careful inquiry who the honest lawyers are, or better still, get a referral, because you need them for **everything**.

Superficial politeness and courtesy on a personal level are very important: greetings and farewells include hand shaking and claps on the shoulder or arm between males and a kiss on one cheek between males and females. Other terms of courtesy include "por favor" and "gracias," "con permiso" (asking permission), "con mucho gusto" (with great pleasure) the response to "gracias." Never walk into a room without greeting everybody there or saying "hasto luego" when you leave. "Pura Vida" (literally translated as "pure life") is the most common and enthusiastic greeting between Ticos.

When it comes to business appointments or when you are expecting somebody to meet you at your house, Costa Ricans frequently simply do not show up or even phone to cancel the appointment. For example, my husband Martin arrived at the doctor's office in San Jose for an appointment. He arrived there – there was no doctor to be found. The doctor was sick and nobody had notified us. This is an extremely frustrating characteristic for most foreigners to deal with. It is as if your time is unimportant, and it does not matter that you may have waited all day in vain. They will never admit that they do not know something, nor will they ever say "No." So if, for example, you make an appointment at 9 a.m. and they show up at 1 p.m., it is because they already had another appointment at 9 a.m., but did not want to tell you they would not be able to make it! Sound complicated?

Bob and Helen have visited Costa Rica several times for extended visits. They have bought land in Costa Rica, but have not made the decision to actually live here yet:

There has to be give and take each way and we have to accept things the way they are. We have certain cultures and traditions that they may think are crazy and they are so laid back but that's the way it is. They are making great progress. Since we have been coming here so many shopping centres have sprung up, new houses etc. But there is room for improvement such as the roads, some of the social organization such as medical services, the high cost of employment such as social security that should be there but there should be more of a balance regarding payment for the services. Costa Rica needs a profitable economy and it has more going for it with its hydroelectric power, good climate. It should do better than other places.

So there are many advantages here. Foreigners can own businesses in Costa Rica and foreign investment is welcome compared to Mexico where there is a law that no foreigners can own a business.

Another habit practiced throughout Costa Rica is blowing the car horn to get one's attention as they drive up to one's house. Instead of getting out of the car and knocking on the door, you are expected to go to the car! I have also learned that Costa Ricans in general are terrified of dogs. Our quartet of rather benign dachshunds grace our front door most of the time, so most Costa Ricans take one look at them as if they were snarling Rottweilers and will not dare to venture out of their cars! They also have a habit of phoning, asking "who's speaking"(quien habla?) as if they don't know who they called,

43

and then hanging up abruptly without an apology for dialing the wrong number. It is an extraordinary dichotomy between profuse personal politeness and anonymous rudeness.

Although Ticos are friendly to foreigners and one does not sense the resentment felt in other Third World countries, do not expect to be invited into their homes. Tico social life revolves around the family and they do not entertain in the North American fashion. There is little concept of developing friendships. It is for this reason, I think, that so many social clubs for foreigners have sprung up. The alternative is to live in isolation since, in my experience, deep friendships with Ticos rarely occur. We know some Ticos who are only too ready to help us if we need them, yet we have never been invited to their homes, despite the fact they have enjoyed social occasions at our house. It is not intentional, it is simply not a concept in this country. We have to constantly remind ourselves that this is THEIR country and we are the ones who have to adapt not expect them to change their ways.

With the rise of tourism since 1993, insecurity has increased because of the growing crime rate, and there is frustration with the government for not providing strong policing for residents and tourists alike. Corruption in government circles and the business world is rampant and has even reached the banks (namely the collapse of Banco Anglo de Costa Rica).

You can make few inroads with the bureaucracy unless you are prepared to grease palms, making Costa Rica no different than its other Latin American neighbours, except that this country puts on a facade of moral integrity. There is a fundamental dishonesty that is hard to deal with. Stealing is a way of life, whether from one's neighbour, one's boss or one's friend. We have found that theft is so widespread among Costa Ricans that nobody trusts each other. It is probably the single most common reason why foreigners give up and return to their countries of origin rather than try and cope. It becomes difficult to run a business when, at every turn, you are being taken advantage of.

John and Mary:

"The whole utopia of living in this country and everything being beautiful, life being easygoing is a complete non-reality. The people in Costa Rica are very friendly (to your face) but we have since learned that it's a whole other matter in business. If they can, they will take advantage of you and will rip you off any way they can but the people themselves are basically good-hearted." I don't think they realize that stealing is a sin." Apparently the church teaches the people that it's not a sin to steal from somebody who has more than they have. My biggest frustration in trying to do business here is how much corruption and red tape there is. All the equipment we brought into this country was brought in by paying people off because that's the only way we could be competitive with other companies in the same business as we are."

Chapter 3
Travelling to Costa Rica

Passports

Make sure you have a valid passport and make a photocopy of it. Citizens of the United States, Canada and most western European and Latin American countries do not need visas to enter Costa Rica and can stay for 90 days. If you overstay the 90 days, you will have to pay a fine and the amount you pay will depend on the number of days you stay over the limit. For longer stays, you have to apply for an exit visa that will allow you to stay for 30 days more, or you can leave the country for 72 hours and return again for three more months.

From the Posada Mimosa guest book:

Many thanks for your warm hospitality, your inspired setting and the wonderful birds. A memorable but brief visit by which to remember Costa Rica – Pura Vida!

Douglas & Rosemary, Hove, England

If you are unlucky enough to lose your passport (as I did) and you did not make a copy of your latest exit and re-entry into Costa Rica (as I didn't), there is a strong chance you will not be able to leave the country. In my case, the British Embassy said it could issue a passport in two days, but I would have to go to immigration to get confirmation of when I re-entered Costa Rica. All passengers entering by plane are computerized the day after they arrive, but those arriving across the border by car or bus are not, and lists of travellers are sent to central offices only once a week. (P.S. I found my passport so I did not have to do any of the above!)

Currency

The currency of Costa Rica is the "colon" in notes of 10,000, 5,000, 2,000, 1,000, 500, 100 and 50 and it devalues about 20% per year against the US dollar. US dollars (bills must be in perfect condition or they will not be accepted) are accepted everywhere and are exchanged at a fair rate in hotels, shops, and restaurants. However, Canadian dollars are not accepted. To change any currency other than US you first have to go to a large bank which changes it to US and then to Costa Rican colones. Most of the time, prices are quoted in US dollars. Canadian currency and travellers' cheques can be exchanged at some hotels and some banks, but not all of them. Scotiabank now offers full banking services for Canadians and others in Costa Rica.

My advice is to travel with US $ travellers' cheques, credit cards and some cash. The best exchange rates can be found at banks, but be prepared for a lengthy wait, especially on Mondays and Fridays. In the last year, automatic bank machines have sprouted up in main locations, but they do not always work. AVOID MONEYCHANGERS ON THE STREET. Counterfeit US dollars are widespread.

Pre-Travel Health Care

It used to be that all Costa Ricans enjoyed cradle-to-grave healthcare. No person, whether Tico or foreigner was denied emergency care, and everyone was treated without questions about ability to pay. However, we have recently heard of instances where people have been refused medical treatment because they are not on the national health care system (seguro). All employers are responsible for putting their employees on "seguro."

I recommend the Clinica Biblica for foreigners, a private hospital, instead of public hospitals.

We have never taken any medication to prevent malaria since we have been travelling and living here for the past seven years. However, dengue, malaria, cholera and AIDS have recently made an appearance. Malaria is mostly found in the Atlantic Provinces and in the northern counties of San Carlos, Los Chiles and Sarapiqui. The Ministry of Health recommends that adults visiting these areas take two tablets (300 mg) of chloroquine (its trade name is Aralen) once a week, two weeks before arriving and six weeks after leaving. It does not prevent the disease but relieves the symptoms.

Mosquito-borne dengue fever has been the most talked about disease. The best remedy is to avoid mosquito breeding grounds (standing water), use insect repellent, especially at dawn and dusk, and cover up as much as possible. The symptoms of dengue are fever and aching joints. There is no vaccine and no cure, but it is rarely fatal. However, if an individual contracts dengue a second time, it can result in death. Vistitors should check to see that their diphtheria, tetanus and polio shots are up to date.

Before leaving Canada, contact:
The Canadian Society for International Health, 1 Nicholas Street, Suite 1105, Ottawa, Ont. K1N 7B7, tel: (613) 241-5785.

They offer health advice for travel to warm climates and "Information for Canadian Travellers" brochures.

Canadians should not rely on their provincial health insurance to completely cover them in the case of illness. IT IS IMPERATIVE TO TAKE OUT SECONDARY INSURANCE BEFORE YOU LEAVE CANADA. More detailed information on health insurance will be provided in a later chapter.

Important Things to Know

Safety

When travelling, many tourists leave their common sense at home. As we have already said, there has been a rise in violent crime since we first visited in 1987, but Costa Rica is still safer than many other tourist destinations. You will notice that most Costa Rican houses have bars on the windows and guard dogs. The suburb of Escazu, home to many foreigners and wealthy Ticos, has experienced an epidemic of robberies and personal attacks in broad daylight. Our son had his mountain bike stolen from him at knifepoint while he was actually riding it in Escazu! Children have been robbed at bus stops, and it seems the criminals roam the streets with little chance of being caught.

Gangs of young teenagers, called "Chapulines," swarmed victims in San Jose until this year. Now, a new law rules that young people who commit crimes will be treated as adults in the courts and will be jailed up to 10 years for their offences, a definite improvement. I think past President Figueres made a genuine effort to toughen up the country's criminal laws.

We have had no problems during the seven years we have been here, although in the last year there have been more robberies in our little village. We live in the country, an hour from San Jose, and neighbours look out for each other. Criminals seem to do their dirty work in or near a big city so that they can quickly sell the fruits of their crime. But that may be changing: there have been incidents in tourist areas like Manuel Antonio and beach communities like Nosara on the Pacific. Past President Figueres created the "tourist police," who are now stationed in main tourist areas. If you take the following precautions, you should have no problems.

- Avoid wearing gold jewellery, especially necklaces and earrings.

- Avoid carrying large amounts of cash or important documents. Take only one credit card, wear a money pouch and do not carry a purse. If you wear a money pouch, wear it under your clothing so it cannot be seen. My husband wears one under his shirt with nothing in it, and puts his money in his pocket. He leaves the pouch as a decoy because it is easier to snatch a pouch than to get into someone's pocket! He has never been robbed since he's been living here.

- Avoid over-friendly street walkers – they could be pickpockets or muggers. Also, Gringos over 40 are often targeted by Tica women who flatter with their attention but are really only interested in money.

- Don't leave luggage or other possessions unattended in public places (e.g., your car, taxis or buses).

- Don't leave anything of value in a parked car, not even in the trunk.

- Be aware of what is going on around you. It helps to have eyes in the back of your head!

- Don't display wads of money.

- If you live in Costa Rica, do not leave your property unattended. The best security is the presence of someone. Guard dogs can be poisoned; alarm systems are costly, not necessarily effective and can be dis mantled; and guards can be disarmed. An empty house is an open invitation. Our staff sleeps at our house whenever we are away.

- When driving, do not stop for anyone except police who are standing by a patrol car or a police motor bike.

- Always carry a photocopy of your passport, complete with date of entry into the country; leave the original in the safety deposit box at your hotel.

- Before setting out, make sure you know how to get to your destination and arrive before sunset.

- Never pick up hitchhikers.

- Do not camp on isolated beaches. Women should never camp alone or drive at night in isolated areas.

NOTE: There have been recent incidents of attacks on rental cars as they leave car rental agencies. The car has a flat tire, people drive up to "help," and the tourists are robbed. On a more positive note, in our 7 years here we have never suffered a violent incident, nor have any of the hundreds of tourists who have stayed with us: they listened to our advice and were careful. Needless to say, the same rules apply to most countries. The problem with Costa Rica is that tourists get lulled into carelessness because they have heard this is "paradise"!

Police

The transit police are everywhere and frequently stop cars for no apparent reason. We have been stopped twice - once for speeding (I was going 103 km/hr - the speed limit is 90 km on the highway) and I was fined 5,000 colones ($25 US). We were stopped a second time and had to show the car registration, our licence and our passport (perhaps a check for stolen cars).

I had a third brush with police when I crashed into another car at an intersection in San Jose on my third day there – my first ever accident in 40 years of driving! I was on my own in the car, trying to drive and navigate at the same time – a nightmare with so many one-way streets and non-existent direction signs. As soon as the accident happened, the driver of the other car asked me if I was alright and soon a large crowd gathered. I felt totally helpless not having the slightest idea where I was, and having such limited knowledge of Spanish. I happened across an American missionary who translated for me with the police until Payman, the owner of a 4-wheel drive car dealership from whom we rented the car, arrived. Everybody was very civilized. To my horror, I realized I had left my driver's licence at my hotel! The police let me return to my hotel to get my papers without fining me. Eventually, Payman settled everything, and I will be eternally grateful.

Taxes and Tips

Hotels charge 18.45% room tax plus a service charge, resulting in a total of 25% added to your hotel bill. Bed and breakfasts with less than 12 rooms add 13% room tax. Restaurants add 13% tax plus 10% gratuity to your check, so there is no need to tip further unless the service is outstanding. Hotel bellboys should be tipped, but not taxi drivers.

Income Tax

If you are under the impression that Costa Rica is a tax-free paradise, you are mistaken! Although taxes are much less than Canada, there are all kinds of hidden taxes. The principle of territoriality is observed by Costa Rican income tax legislation, meaning that FOREIGN SOURCE INCOME IS EXEMPT. However, everybody residing in Costa Rica is subject to paying tax on property or business income derived from sources in Costa Rica.

Tax rates for personal incomes for the fiscal year 2000 are as follows:

- Employees who earn less than 215,600 colones per month are exempt.

- Income over 215,600 – 324,100 colones is taxed at a rate of 10%.

- Income over 324,100 colones is taxed at a rate of 15%.

- People with their own businesses earning up to 958,000 colones are exempt.

- Income from 958,000 – 1,431,000 is taxed at a rate of 10%.

- Income from 1,431,000 – 2,388,000 is taxed at a rate of 15%.

- Income from 2,388,000 – 4,785,000 is taxed at a rate of 20%.

- Income over 4,785,000 is taxed at a rate of 25%.

These figures are adjusted yearly. There is no capital gains tax on real estate, but the Income Tax Law establishes a conveyance tax at a single rate of 3% of the value of properties valued above 600,000 colones.

Corporation Tax

As of September 1998, gross income from 00.00 to 14,347,000 colones is taxed at a rate of 10% on net income. Gross income from 14,347,000 to 28,860,000 colones is taxed 20% on net income and gross income over 28,860,000 colones is taxed 30%.

Social Security Taxes For Employers

Employers pay 22% taxes on the gross salary paid monthly to their employees. For example, on a payroll with gross salaries totaling 1,000,000 colones, an employer pays 220,000 colones plus 9% deducted from employees' salary.

Property Taxes

Property taxes are approximately 0.25% a year on the value of the property, according to the municipality's appraisal. Tax bills are paid in March and can be paid by your lawyer. Garbage tax is approximately $10 US per month.

Tax bills are not sent out by the municipalities. The onus is on the individual property owner to find out how much tax they owe. If you have not paid your taxes, you do not receive a reminder. Instead, a fine is added to the outstanding tax bill. We did not know the routine when we first arrived and found out, to our surprise, we owed two and a half years of back taxes plus fines!

Sales Tax

There is a 13% tax on products and services, and a consumption tax of 15% on locally produced or imported luxury goods. Taxes on alcohol and cigarettes increased in January 2000. A 2 litre bottle of Nikolai vodka now costs 4,075 colones (313 colones = $1 October 2000). The estimated $32 million in revenue will go to social institutions that cater to the elderly and children at risk.

Christmas Bonus, Vacation Pay and Severance

Employers are required to pay a Christmas bonus of one month's pay every year and two weeks' vacation pay a year to employees who have worked for more than three months. In the case of termination of employment, the employer has to pay one month's pay for every year the employee has worked, up to an 8-year limit. Workmen's Compensation Insurance is mandatory and is 3.4% on gross payroll.

Home Help

Home help is more expensive than it was two years ago, but is still inexpensive when compared to North America. For example, our office assistant, who doubles as a handyman, earns 30,000 colones week ($80). Our part-time maids work 5 hours a day, 6 days a week and earn 12,000 colones ($30). Our full-time gardener earns 25,000 colones a week. The average monthly minimum wage is about $200-$300. Every 6 months, employees who earn minimum wage receive an increase of 4.58% to keep abreast of inflation. Every December, employers pay "aguinaldo," a bonus for the thirteenth month, to employees who have been on the job for a year or more. They are also entitled to two weeks paid vacation.

When hiring people, it is prudent to employ them on a trial basis for 3 months. After three months, they can make claims against employers who fire them, resulting in a costly, tiresome battle. The most important quality to look for in employees is honesty. If you find an honest employee who is not as efficient as you would like, keep him or her. Honest workers in Costa Rica are a valuable commodity.

We recently had to fire one of our maids whom we suspected of stealing: our first and only experience with theft. Even when an employee is suspected of theft, the employer still has to pay a bonus and holiday pay, as well as notice and severance pay! Our maid went to the Ministry of Labour and came back with a letter saying we owed her 129,000 colones. We went to our lawyer, who said we should give her a letter from us to take to the Ministry in which we said she had violated Code # such and such of the Labour Code. Since she did not take the letter to the Ministry, we did. They said she was only entitled to holiday pay and a bonus that amounted to 28,000 colones! A significant reduction from what she had originally wanted. We paid her by cheque and had her sign a receipt saying this was her final payment to protect ourselves from further claims.

Most people have maids who do not live in. The maid we inherited when we bought our property has worked at the house for 15 years and treats it as her own. There are all kinds of people available to do yard work and other maintenance at very low costs.

John and Mary:

"I think that employees look upon a foreigner running a business here as somebody who should pay them more or give them something extra because they think we have more to begin with. The main problem I have found with Costa Rican workers is that their focus is for today not the long-term picture. Consequently, if they can cheat you out of one or two hours a day by driving the truck slower or by saying that they have a problem that needs to be fixed, their focus will be just to put in time to make money for the day. So we have to educate them that the company's interests come first because if they don't, then they will have no jobs. You have to have eyes in the back of your head. I don't think they will blatantly take a lot but they take a little all the time."

Mail and Telephone

Mail service to Canada and within the country is more reliable than we first thought. Overseas mail can take from 10 days to over two weeks, and mail is only occasionally lost. Do not send cheques or money by mail. When sending gifts, especially CDs or video-casssettes, do not write on the outside that they are enclosed, to avoid possible theft. Many expats maintain a post box in Miami, Florida for mail forwarding, but Federal Express, through a company called Jetex, now offers door-to-door service. We previously had to go to their office in San Jose to pick up packages. DHL has just opened offices here as well and, even better, UPS has an office in Grecia. Because there are no street names or home delivery service, most residents pick up their mail at the post office. With the increased use of fax machines and E-mail, we receive less and less mail.

Apartado and the abbreviation Apdo means post office box (P.O. Box)

Telephones are hard to come by, and it may take two years or more to get one. If you do not pay your telephone bill on time, your phone will be immediately cut off – very frustrating! The same happens if you do not pay your electric bill on time. Generally speaking, the telephone service is good, and we are connected to Internet and E-mail. Ordering our second telephone line was a very complicated procedure, and included getting a form signed and notarized by our lawyer. The process was made more difficult because we could not understand what the telephone people were asking us to do! The extra line cost 39,500 colones in 1994 and took 6 months to get. We applied for a phone for another house on our property over two years ago (1998), and it was finally installed in November 2000!

Packing and Moving

There is a real sense of finality when you actually move all your worldly goods to another country. We were determined not to take along boxes of accumulated objects that

58

were never re-opened or missed. When you are making a break with one way of life and starting a completely new chapter, you want to eliminate the superfluous. Our move from our big house to a condo in May 1993 was by far the most difficult because a lot of sorting and organizing had to be done. This time, the moving company did most of the work.

We called Global International, a company recommended by friends who had already moved to Costa Rica. We had to complete a detailed inventory with the value of each article. The company moves everything from door to door, and has an agent in Costa Rica who does all the paper work and gets things through customs. Since most of our belongings were used and we were not taking appliances or new electronic items, we did not have too difficult a time. The only new articles we took were drapes and duvet covers I had made in Oakville, Ontario, towels and sheets and the necessary hardware to go with the drapes.

To quote from a government handout, "there is an exemption from all tariffs and surtaxes which apply to the importation or local purchase of those articles which are indispensable to the function or installation of new enterprises." We figured that drapes and bedding should fall under "hotel services," one of the tourism investment categories. We took a 40 foot container and, at the last minute, Martin gave me nightmares because he said a 40 foot container would not be able to go down our new driveway! Global reassured us that they would shuttle our belongings with smaller trucks (adding to the cost).

When evaluating goods, our son recommended we put a realistic price on things, and then there is less chance of a hassle at Customs. New appliances, electric and electronic devices are the most likely targets for paying high duties, as well as cars. We decided against taking our cars and appliances because of this.

NOTE: Christmas is a bad time to move because the port at Limon is closed for the holidays from December 22 until after New Year's.

If you are planning to move internationally, I highly recommend Global. Their phone number is (905) 475-1990; Fax: (905) 475-9542.

Chapter 4
Getting To and Getting Around Costa Rica
When To Go

Costa Rica is an ideal winter destination for North Americans and Europeans because the seasons are reversed. The dry season or summer, which lasts from December to May, is the best time to visit as it coincides with the dreariest weather in northern climes. The rainy season or winter runs from mid-May till the end of November, with September and October being the wettest months. We find that the countryside looks its most beautiful at the end of November when everything is still emerald-green and the sugar cane is blooming. During the dry season in the Central Valley, the temperature is consistently warm and varies from 70 - 90 F, with cool breezes making it pleasant and comfortable. There is no need for expensive air conditioning; ceiling fans suffice. On the Atlantic coast it rains year round, and on the Pacific coast it is extremely hot and humid all year.

From the Posada Mimosa guest book:

I don't think I'll ever forget my first view of the Southern Cross pointed out by Martin or the view from our breakfast table.

Nan & Pat,
Fort Wayne, Indiana

Bob and Helen:

"We came to look, we liked it, we bought a lot, we could have built a house and stayed here forever, move down completely. We lived in the Arctic for a long time so it is quite a change. Helen has always wanted to retire to the tropics close to The Equator where the only problem was a coconut falling on her head!"

During the rainy season, mornings are usually sunny and it starts clouding over around noon with downpours in the afternoon and some evenings. We find it very refreshing when it rains, and the music of the rain on the metal roofs is somehow soothing and reassuring. There is no need for streets to be cleaned. Nature washes them every day, and the flowers and tropical foliage are so lush and abundant. The mountains are emerald green, dotted with coffee plantations. If you plan to sightsee during the rainy season, you must do it first thing in the morning, before the afternoon rains come. About the only thing predictable about Costa Rica is the weather! The government is trying to encourage the development of the "green" season. They want to target select groups such as surfers, windsurfers, kayakers and sports fishermen who do not necessarily rely on the weather to enjoy Costa Rica.

Certainly, the dry season is the best time to go, but the rainy season is not at all unpleasant and should not be ruled out. In fact, more people (especially Europeans) are visiting during June, July and August when children are on their school holidays. Americans from the southern states come to the cool mountains to escape their summer heat. But many more should discover that going south to the tropical mountains can be much cooler than Florida, Texas or Washington in July and August. The first two weeks of July are called "little summer" because it rarely rains at that time.

Flights

Canadians are luckier than most because they can fly directly and non-stop from Toronto and Montreal to Costa Rica with several charter airlines organized by *Canadian Holidays, Conquest, Signature Vacations, Alba Tours, Sun*

Quest, Air Transat and Canada 3000. Most charters run from the beginning of November until the end of April, except service to Liberia that begins December 20. *Air Transat* runs charter flights out of Montreal from November-May. Prices and departures change constantly. The Costa Rican national airline, *LACSA*, operates three flights a week from Toronto via Havana. You cannot use frequent flyer points on charter flights. *Martinair* and *LTU* have charters in the high season from Germany. *IBERIA* also operates flights from Madrid. All of the European charters have stops on the way.

Getting Around

Driving in Costa Rica is a hair-raising experience! Not only do you have to watch out for crazy drivers, you have to keep your eyes glued to the road to avoid the giant pot-holes waiting to swallow you up, car and all! Cars zigzag along the highway, attempting to avoid potholes, looking like so many drunken drivers. Tourists and residents alike complain more about the state of the roads than anything else. I must add that since the new government was elected in 1999, the roads have definitely improved, especially the signs. The main road to Grecia is probably the best in the country.

Costa Ricans, who are normally peaceful and polite, display a maniacal disregard for human or beast behind the wheel. Pedestrians cross the road at their peril, blissfully ignoring the smoke-belching vehicles bearing down on them. Nobody signals, everybody ignores signals, nobody will let you in, the horn reigns supreme, and the smaller the vehicle, the more hazardous it is. Buses and trucks rule, and the pecking order goes on down from largest to smallest. My conclusion is that Ticos feel that behind the

wheel of a car, they at last have some power and control –
they are in charge! It is a perfectly understandable senti-
ment in this maddeningly bureaucratic society, where the
individual feels powerless most of the time, waits in endless lines to do the simplest transaction and is controlled
by inept politicians.

Taxis

IF POSSIBLE, DO NOT DRIVE IN SAN JOSE: TAKE A TAXI.
There are two types of taxis – the legally licensed ones
that display their licences on the door and the illegal ones
that display no licence number. These are "pirate" taxis.
Both types are red, so it is easy to confuse them. All taxis
are required to run the meter with each fare. However,
even the licensed taxis try and get away with not putting
them on. Each time you get into a taxi, ensure the meter
is on by saying to the driver "para maria." If he does not
put it on, ask the people at your destination how much the
fare should be and pay that amount. It is always a good
idea to find out how much the fare is before getting into
the taxi. Nevertheless, taxis are very, very, cheap and
plentiful, except when it rains!

Car Rentals

Car rentals are not cheap and are often in short supply,
especially four-wheel drive vehicles in the high season.
Canadians can lease and pay for car rentals in Canada
before they leave home and pick up their car at the airport here. This also applies to other countries. *Thrifty* has
been used by most of our clients, but there are other
equally good companies such as *Economy, Budget, Avis*
and *Hertz.*

Some car rental companies charge hefty deposits (as much as $1,000) on your credit card, leaving you that much less credit available during your holiday. When booking, be sure to check if they charge a deposit and ask EXACTLY what the insurance covers. Some credit cards say they cover car insurance worldwide and there is no need to take out extra insurance. However, some of our clients have experienced problems with some local car rental agencies that sell their own additional insurance. Be sure to check when you book.

It is better to deal with the well-known agencies rather than smaller companies because the cars are in better condition, the service is more reliable, and you can pick up and drop off cars at the airport. Some of our clients have experienced frustration with some companies when their cars were not ready for pickup, or they were told a car was not available even though they had booked their cars in advance. If you do rent a car, be sure to check the vehicle thoroughly before accepting it. Look at the tires (including the spare), windshield wipers, lights, air-conditioning (if you asked for it), motor and body. If you notice any dents or scratches point them out so you won't be charged for them later. Some people take videos of the car before they start driving.

If you plan to do adventurous driving off the main highway, it is better to lease a car with four-wheel drive to negotiate the difficult secondary roads and explore off the beaten track. I have also heard that car rental agencies will not rent standard cars unless you promise you will not drive on unpaved roads!

If you drive in San Jose, park your car in special parking garages (parqueos) that are guarded and secure. Car theft, like elsewhere in the world, is a roaring business. If you do not want to lease a car or drive yourself, you can hire a car and driver – the cost of $60 a day is about the same as that of a car rental, with none of the worries. The cost increases depending on distance.

> If you are not already a member of the CAA, join before you leave Canada. Their affiliate club in Costa Rica is THE AUTOMOBILE CLUB OF COSTA RICA, Apartado P.O. 4646, San Jose, C.R. 1000; tel:(506)220-04-43.
>
> CAA also offers one of the best health insurances policies.

Purchasing a Car

If you decide to move to Costa Rica, a car is a must. New cars are very expensive and are excellent targets for thieves. We decided to buy second-hand cars that actually appreciate in value! We bought a 1983 Volkswagen Rabbit ($3000 US), a 1988 Isuzu Trooper 4WD ($11,000 US) and a 1985 15-seater Toyota bus ($13,000 US).

Supplementary insurance is optional and covers personal liability. Mandatory insurance for all vehicles is renewed automatically every year along with the license tags for $25 -$35 a year, for which you get a windshield sticker called a "marchamo." It covers injury to third parties in an accident involved with the insured vehicle. However, the limits are low and range from $1100 per person to $5,000 per death per accident.

> For more information, read Insurance in Costa Rica by David R. Garrett.
> tel: (506) 233-2455; fax: (506) 222 0007.

Why three vehicles for two people? Because one or another is always in the garage! Cars take a tremendous beating on the roads, so it is very important to have a good mechanic (few and far between). The hassle of changing ownership, getting a car registered and licence is a time-consuming process best left to your lawyer to handle. After 6 years, we finally received the license plates for one of our vehicles!

Shipping a Car

We do not recommend shipping a new American or European car because:

(1) most cars here are Japanese made and parts are not readily available for other makes or they are more costly.

(2) you will have to pay 100% duty:

(3) by the time you pay for the shipping, the duty, registration in the public registry, the services of a lawyer to get you through a very complicated process, it is far simpler to buy a used car here (although even that is a frustrating exercise!).

If you bring in your car as a tourist, you will be issued a three-month permit that can be extended to six months. At the end of the six months, you have to leave the country with your car or pay the taxes. Every foreigner is considered a tourist unless he/she has residency status.

Driving Tips

Driving in Costa Rica is a challenge and an adventure. We thought we would never have the nerve to do it, but found that by driving aggressively and not defensively, we survived (being ex-Montrealers was a decided advantage!).

- Arm yourself with a good, clear up-to-date map. Some maps do not have new roads marked on them.

- Before you leave on your trip, book accommodation at your destination, especially in the high season (December-April).

- Plan to arrive before sunset. Driving after dark is difficult. The sun sets between 5.30 p.m. and 6 p.m. all year round. Days start early, so if you are not a morning person, you soon will be.

- Be alert at all times to the many hazards crossing your path: pedestrians, animals lying nonchalantly on roads, pavement that suddenly ends, potholes, unlit vehicles (particularly bicycles which never have lights), motor scooters (a real menace), sudden fog in mountainous areas, torrential rains and reckless drivers.

- Since 1993, the transit police seem to have eased up on stopping cars for no apparent reason. Cars are usually stopped for licence checks, seatbelts, speeding, or passing on a double line. If stopped, you are only obliged to show a copy of your passport and stamp of entry, driver's licence and registration. In the past, some police officers asked for bribes, but police are now paid more so this is not as prevalent.

- Never leave anything of value in a parked car, even if it's locked, even in the trunk.

Chapter 5
Where To Go and What To See

Before you book your trip, decide on your main reason for going: Adventure sports? Nature and jungle trekking? Volcanoes? Beach holiday? Seeing as much of the country as possible? Learning Spanish and getting to know the people? Being close to San Jose to access consultants or lawyers to learn more about living and retiring in Costa Rica? This country is beautiful and diverse and, even though it is small, it takes more time than you think to go from one place to another. You really have to do your homework before leaving, otherwise time passes too quickly and you will not get the most out of your trip.

From the Posada Mimosa guest book:

We discussed together the expression "highlights of life"- Posada Mimosa is one of our highlights – thank you for your great hospitality!

Cora & Robert, Mallorca, Spain

Where To Stay

San Jose, the capital, is indistinguishable from other Latin American cities. It is an ugly hodgepodge of architectural styles, noisy, and badly polluted because of increasing traffic. Petty thievery has turned into daring armed robberies and knife attacks over the last three years. I always feel sorry for package tourists who spend their first night there, creating a terrible first impression of Costa Rica. If you must stay in San Jose, our favourite small hotel is the *Hotel Grano de Oro* run by a Canadian couple from Saskatchewan who moved to Costa Rica about ten years ago. They moved back to Canada in 1996 but still own the hotel. It is full most of the year and, in a short time, has gained the reputation of being one of the best small hotels in Costa Rica.

Unfortunately, the Canadian charters all book their package tours into large, impersonal international style hotels like the *Hotel Irazu, San Jose Palacio* (a favourite for European tour groups), and *Hotel Corobici.* The *Hotel Cariari* and *Hotel Bougainvillea* are more Costa Rican in decor and ambiance. The Bougainvillea is 10 minutes outside of San Jose and is owned by a Dutchman who has been in Costa Rica for over 35 years. His hobbies are art collecting and gardening – the garden is glorious and every wall of the hotel is filled with interesting paintings from all over the world, as well as Costa Rican and pre-Columbian artifacts. There is an hourly shuttle bus that takes you back and forth to San Jose. The *Bougainvillea* has a swimming pool and tennis courts so if you enjoy peace and quiet, it is the place to be. The dining room service and food are both excellent.

Homestays

If large hotels are not your cup of tea and you are the adventurous type, there are plenty of alternative accommodations listed on the Internet. Another option for accommodation in San Jose is homestays.

HOMESTAYS with a Tico family can be a wonderful cross-cultural exchange and a great insight into Costa Rican life, as well as the best way to learn Spanish. We met a couple from Texas at a local language school who were staying with a family with their two young children, 18 months and 5 years. The family looked after the children while they attended school and even offered to baby sit while they went travelling! Ticos adore children. If you do decide to stay with a family, be prepared for small houses, shared facilities, little privacy (Ticos' sense of privacy and space are poles apart from a North American perspective), and a much higher noise level than most foreigners are used to (e.g., barking dogs, constant chatter, loud music and traffic).

Vernon and Marcela Bell of Bell's Home Hospitality have organized homestays in suburban San Jose since 1990. Rates are $30 single, $45 double per day and an extra $5 per day for a private bathroom, including breakfast. Optional dinners cost $7 per meal and airport pickup costs $15 for the first person and $5 for each additional person. Contact Bell's Home Hospitality at Dept. 1432, P.O. Box 025216, Miami, Fla 33102 or Apdo. 185, San Jose 1000; tel: 225-4752, fax: 224-5884. e-mail: homestay@racsa.co.co; website: www.homestay.thebells.org

What To See

There is so much to see in Costa Rica, and some roads are in such poor shape, it takes three or four times longer than you expect to get from A to B. However, there have recently been some improvements. For example, the road from *Puntarenas* to *Flamingo Beach* is in excellent shape, but once at the beach, the road is really rutted and in the rainy season is washed out altogether. When we first visited twelve years ago, there were also no direction signs along the way – that has greatly improved in the last couple of years.

Getting Directions

There are still no street names or addresses (rather like Tokyo), so getting directions to go anywhere requires lengthy descriptions of distance and landmarks to reach the desired address. For example, imagine you stop and ask a Tico how to get to the car rental agency. They are only too delighted to help, and in rapid Spanish will tell you to go 200 metres north, turn left, go 150 metres until you come to XYZ building, turn right, go 400 more metres and you will see a garage on the right, a Toyota dealership on the left, go 50 more metres and voila, there's your car rental agency! (For people like me with absolutely no concept of metre measurement, it took a while to learn that 100 metres = one block.) Or, if you ask a Tico for directions to a town and he does not know the way, there will be a conference with two or three other equally unsure people, resulting in totally incorrect directions, or you might even be told to "follow that bus!" Costa Ricans really do want to help, but are unable to say they do not know the answer to something.

Highlights of Our First Trip

If you are a first time visitor to Costa Rica, one week is really not enough. However, we have had a number of guests who did a lot in a week and went home refreshed and renewed. Two weeks is better. On our first visit in 1987, we stayed the first week near San Jose at the *Hotel Cariari*, which has an 18-hole golf course, 10 tennis courts, a swimming pool and Costa Rican decor. It is a good spot to take side trips from. Since that time, many new hotels have sprung up. As mentioned before, on our first visit we went on a package tour. Most tours include hotel and air fare, and side trips can be arranged upon arrival. We spent our second week at the *Flamingo Hotel* on the Pacific coast in *Guanacaste* province. It is very hot and humid there, sapping all one's energy.

Six years ago there was very little development, but today development and land values have soared.

Turtle Safari

The highlight of our first visit was a "turtle safari," when our guide took us in a jeep at 1 a.m. to observe the giant turtles lumbering up the beach to lay their eggs. They can only be viewed at night under a moonless sky. We were all equipped with flashlights as we silently tiptoed along the beach, searching out turtles. There was many a giggle at the sight of all these tourists creeping around the beach in the middle of the night! But we were rewarded, and what a sight it was to see the turtles do as they have done for thousands of years. It was truly awesome, though sad to know that so few of those newly hatched turtles will survive, as predators of all kinds snatch them before they even reach the ocean.

Four years ago, the National Parks Service imposed rules restricting when people can be on the area's beaches, and prohibiting them from carrying cameras. Even turtles like to lay their eggs in peace, without dozens of flashes blitzing their posteriors! We recently visited *Hotel Las Tortugas*, right on *Playa Grande* where the turtles start nesting in October and do so until February. The hotel specializes in nature groups and surfers. Louis, the owner, is a charming American who has lived in Costa Rica for over 25 years and is a pioneer in nature tourism. He works closely with *Earth Watch*, an environmental group that monitors the turtles on *Playa Grande*.

Several of our guests have highly recommended *Hotel Capitano Suizo and El Jardin de Eden* in nearby *Tamarindo*. We liked *Hotel Sugar Beach* in the *Flamingo* area for its peace and quiet. *"Sueno del Mar"* is a charming bed and breakfast right on the beach in *Tamarindo*.

Manuel Antonio National Park

Avoid *Jaco Beach* – it is full of tourists, the sand is black, and the ocean is dangerous for swimming, resulting in drownings. There are no lifeguards and few caution notices. But, if you like an active nightlife, there are many bars and restaurants. On the way to *Manuel Antonio*, do not miss visiting nearby *Carara Biological Reserve*, famous for its scarlet macaws. Before you get to the Reserve, there is a bridge where you can stop and see huge crocodiles basking in the sun.

Manuel Antonio National Park has 3 beautiful white sandy beaches with the jungle on one side and the Pacific on the other. The park itself is 1,685 acres, with hundreds of beautiful species of plants. Hike the trails or go by horse-back, surf, swim, snorkel or simply laze on the beaches. The best times to go to the park to see the most wildlife is early in the morning or in the late afternoon. Animals, being the sensible creatures they are, generally have the good sense to sleep at noon, the hottest time of day!   Nearby *Quepos* is an old-time fishing and banana town only 4 km away from the park. There is plentiful and excellent accommodation in all price ranges. The highway between *Jaco* and *Parrita* is now in very good shape (after years of having unsuspecting motorists confronted by car-eating potholes).

Other Places To Go

Don't miss the *Cabo Blanco Reserve*, Costa Rica's oldest protected wildlife region, the *Monteverde Cloud Forest* (beware of the appalling roads!), *Los Angeles Cloud Forest* (a better road and less crowded than *Monteverde*), the volcanoes and the *Lake Arenal* region with its thermal baths, *Smithsonian Observatory* and the most active volcano on earth. *Corcovado National Park* in the south is a "tropical wet forest" teeming with biological diversity and endangered wildlife. Five hundred species of trees, 10,000 insects, hundreds of species of birds, frogs, lizards, turtles and spectacular mammals live there. Biological stations and wilderness camps abound. There is so much to see and do in Costa Rica, make sure you pick and choose carefully according to your particular interests.

Highlights of Our Second Trip

On our second visit to Costa Rica in November 1993, we went to *Playa Samara* on the *Nicoya Peninsula.* We had a chance to experience the transition between the dry and rainy seasons. It is about a 4-hour drive from *Santa Ana* over bone-shattering roads, so we decided to fly instead – a mere 40 minutes. Unfortunately, the 40-minute flight with *Sansa Airlines* took about 4 hours! We had to go in to San Jose to buy the tickets at their office, and discovered they accepted only US dollars. (Now they take credit cards as well.) The cost is about $50 US one-way and $100 US return for tourists; Costa Ricans pay half. This double price standard can really frustrate visitors when they discover that they are often charged double because they are tourists.

On our flight to *Samara* in a 22-seater plane, we stopped first at *Tamarindo*, then *Nosara* and finally *Samara*. The dirt landing strip is in the middle of nowhere, right next to a beautiful white, sandy beach with hardly a soul on it. We were deposited with our baggage and a man came up to us, nodding and smiling. He turned out to be the airlines local rep, baggage handler, air controller, check-in (out) agent, cow chaser to clear the runway and storyteller while we waited on a rock in the shade of palm trees! Then in the distance, we spotted a cloud of dust enveloping what looked like our son Jason's blue Toyota as it sped up the landing strip to pick us up. Out he jumped with newly sprouting beard, beaming from ear to ear, looking every inch the beach bum!

We definitely recommend flying to the beaches. It is at least a 4-hour drive from San Jose over roads less than perfect. Travelair offers flights every day including Sundays and holidays, both to the Caribbean and Pacific coasts. Round trip fares from December to April cost from $72 to $136, depending on your destination. Children under two years of age fly free, from 2 to 12 pay half fare. Flights leave from Pavas airport.
Reservations can be made by fax with a credit card.
Reservations - Tel: 220-3054; Fax: 220-0413.
Sansa Airlines does not go to as many destinations as Travelair and not all flights are daily. The cost is more or less the same.
Reservations - Tel: 221-9414

We stayed at the *Villas Playa Samara*. There are 90 one-bedroom, two-bedroom and three- bedroom villas right on the beach, set in lush tropical surroundings. The villas are sold and then leased out. French-Canadians own the property, and it fits nicely into the environment. There is a dining room, pool, bar, tennis courts and disco and howler monkeys in a tree near the villas! There is absolutely nothing to do except walk miles of sandy beaches and enjoy safe swimming in the ocean. If you are on a honeymoon or really want to relax and do nothing, this is the place for you. On a scale of one to five stars, I would rate it a three-star by Costa Rican standards.

VillasPlaya Samara:
The cost per night is Rooms ($102), villas ($141-$272/2-6 people).
Tel: (506) 656-0100; Fax: 656-0109

There is cheaper accommodation in this area: rooms can be rented for $28 a night if you do not mind sharing a bathroom.

While on the *Nicoya Peninsula*, try to stay at or visit the 30-room *Hotel Tango Mar*, a beach resort and country club that feels like a seaside inn. You can play golf to the sound of the ocean. This is definitely for the high end of the market. The resort arranges trips to *Cabo Blanco Wildlife Preserve* on the tip of the peninsula, with monkeys, birds and orange-and-purple crabs. Horseback riding is also available.

> *Hotel Tango Mar:*
> *Rooms ($155); suites ($169-$214); villas ($950) includes breakfast.*
> *Tel: (506) 683-0001; Fax: 683-0003*

If you prefer beach to jungle, book the *Hotel El Ocotal* at the northernmost point on the Nicoya.

Manuel Antonio & Quepos

We decided we wanted to see more Pacific beaches, so we set off by car on the 4-hour trip to *Manuel Antonio* and *Quepos*. The scenery was spectacular as we wound our way through steep hairpin turns. As we neared *Quepos*, the condition of the roads deteriorated. We literally slalomed around the potholes, laughing as we watched oncoming traffic careening all over the road in an effort to avoid wrecking their vehicles! It was quite a challenge! The condition of the road has improved since our first visit. We finally arrived at our destination in pouring rain!

We decided to go out to dinner right away rather than unpack the car (not a good idea in Costa Rica!). We went

> *We stayed at El Lirio, a small hotel run by a Canadian named Kathy Young. It cost us $35 a night (in the low season) for a comfortable, clean room set in lush surroundings with a big pool. In the high season, which starts at the beginning of December, the rate is $55-double and $65-triple a night, with a continental breakfast. Tel: (506) 777-0403; Fax: 777-1182.*

77

to *La Barba Roja* nearby and parked our car right near the hotel entrance. Halfway through dinner, our waiter told us that somebody had seen someone trying to get into the trunk of our car! The police were called and nothing had been stolen, even though we had left our front door unlocked by mistake and the trunk could easily have been opened. Make sure to unload your car as soon as you arrive at your destination and do not leave anything on the seats. Our car had the name of the rental car company on it and the licence plate had the letters TUR. Taking a cue from Florida, rental cars are now no longer easily identifiable.

Quepos

Downtown *Quepos* is not very attractive. Many small new hotels have sprung up along the beaches outside of the town in the past three years. The government is trying to keep hotels no higher than palm trees. Until 1995, *La Mariposa* hotel was the queen of them all. It is perched on a hill with a 360-degree breathtaking panoramic view of the Pacific. It has 10 rooms that are terraced, independent two floor villas consisting of a bedroom with two double beds and living room and eating area downstairs. It enjoys 100% occupancy most of the time. We went there for lunch and luckily enjoyed the view before the fog and rain rolled in. A French family owns the hotel, and before coming to Costa Rica they owned hotels in St. Maarten and Venezuela. It is well worth a visit for a leisurely meal.

La Mariposa now has competition with the opening of *El Parador*, owned and managed by Dutch people. It is quite

La Mariposa:
Villas ($136-$200), gourmet restaurant.
Tel: 506-777-0456; fax: 506-777-0050

different than any other hotel I have seen here. It too is perched on a point and has an equally splendid view. The rooms are beautifully decorated and the main hotel is filled with Dutch antiques. We stayed there when it had just opened and they were still building condos. Large pool, tennis, miniature golf, helicopter landing pad, airport, restaurants.

El Parador:
Rooms ($173-$220); suites ($315); presidential suite ($844) including breakfast.
Tel: 506-777-1411; fax: 506-777-1437

Manuel Antonio Park

The government finally "rectified mistakes," and reduced park entrance fees for non-residents from $15 to $6. However, residents and Costa Ricans still only pay 200 colones. There was such widespread criticism of the former fees that attendance at the parks dropped dramatically and the length of time tourists stayed in the country decreased. At the same time, the agreement also included a reduction in hotel rates and taxes on tourism, the country's number one source of foreign revenue. In return, hotels agreed to lower their advertised package rates by 15 percent.

We went to *Manuel Antonio Park* (closed on Mondays), right on the beach. Although there are guided tours, we decided to go it on our own. To get to the park entrance, you have to wade through a lagoon of knee-high water. We recommend that you wear flip-flops and a bathing suit under shorts so that you can enjoy a swim. There are no changing rooms in the area.

We happened across a French photographer who was taking pictures for Italian and French nature magazines, and wherever he stopped, so did we. We saw very tame white-faced monkeys playing in the trees at water's edge. They have amazingly human-like faces and are quite a treat to watch as they play and swing from tree to tree. Perhaps the most interesting animal we saw was a three-toed sloth that moved in slow motion up and down the trees. Apparently sloths only move three or four times a day, so we were incredibly lucky to see one in action – although action is probably not the word to describe the unbelievably slow progress it makes. We also spotted a female sloth with a baby clinging to her high up in the trees - a dark, inert, motionless mass. We saw plenty of iguanas, but not many birds. We must admit that we saw much more animal and bird life in the *Carara Biological Reserve*. If you hire a guide you get the most out of a park visit.

Arenal Volcano

Arenal Volcano is a pleasant change from the beaches. We stayed overnight in Fortuna and took a four-hour boat trip on the *Rio Frio in Las Chiles*, 20 km from the Nicaraguan border. We passed through three police checks on the way. I asked what they were looking for and they said "people" (read Nicaraguans) and "drugs." We saw a wonderful assortment of birds - roseate spoonbills, aninjas, toucans, green herons, great blue herons, ibizes, egrets, scarlet tanagers, kingfishers and storks, to name just a few. We also saw Jesus Christ lizards (they walk on water!), howler monkeys, caymans (small crocodiles) and iguanas. We met a couple who added 60 new birds to their list during their trip. They highly recommend *Monteverde* for avid birders. They recommended staying at *El Sapo Dorado*. It has separate cabins with fireplaces.

If you do visit *Monteverde*, be prepared for the absolutely worst road, taking one hour and a half of rattling and shaking to go 30 km from the main highway. When we reached our destination, we asked why something is not done to improve the roads. Apparently there was a vote among the inhabitants, and they all agreed to keep the roads the way they were so that they would not be over-run by tourists!

Once again, it took us longer than two hours to get to *Arenal* over tortuous alpine roads. The final road to *Arenal Lodge* surpassed any we had ever come across, and we were surprised we made it without a four-wheel drive vehicle. We had a huge room facing the volcano that was bathed in the light of a full moon. I was mesmerized by the brooding presence of the volcano as it spewed red lava down its face and fussed and fumed as it released its gases. It is much more dramatic viewing the volcano at night. The next morning we were awoken by a rather angry howler monkey bellowing his disapproval of anyone being near his trees – and heaven help you if you are! They have been known to very accurately aim their excre-ment on the heads of unsuspecting tourists!

Since we were there three years ago, a lot of attractive bed and breakfasts have sprung up. Our guests highly recommend Villa Decary in Nuevo Arenal, however you do not have a view of the volcano. Rates are $67 - $78, includes breakfast. Tel: 506-38e3-3012; fax: 506-694-4330

Lake Arenal

On our way back to San Jose, we stopped at *Tabuchon* resort near *Lake Arenal*. It has thermal hot springs that include swimming pools and cascading waterfalls that

81

massage you as you sit under them. It is a wonderful place to go after jouncing around the roads or doing strenuous bike riding. They also have very good food and outstandingly beautiful gardens. Two years ago, they opened a hotel offering full services. Nearby Lake Arenal has excellent sports fishing and windsurfing for experts, and its mysterious quality reminded us of Loch Ness in Scotland. Unfortunately, fickle winds, rain and choppy waters often interfere with fishing and windsurfing.

Montana del Fuego in La Fortuna is another place to stay that has been recommended by some of our clients. Wooden bungalows ($67). Tel: 506-460-1220; fax: 506-460-1455. Tel/Fax 479-9004.

Cabinas Paraiso, close to Tabuchon, faces the volcano and offers clean, rustic cabins at half the price of Tabuchon. ($25-$60).

Other Sites

We also visited *Puerto Viejo* and *Cajuita* during one of our trips, and drove through Limon on the Atlantic coast. We were a little disappointed, expecting much more charm and ambiance. The white sandy beaches were unspoilt and the pretty drive took us all down the coast. It came as a surprise that English was so widely spoken.

In October 1996 and 1997, we followed our son as he took part in "*la Ruta de Conquistadores*," an annual 3-day, 500 km international mountain biking race from *Puntarenas* on the Pacific to *Limon* on the Atlantic coast. The competitors follow the same route as the Spanish conquerors. It was an extremely gruelling race, and the 80 participants earned our utmost respect. We were pleased that Jason came about 26th in the field! It was a great chance to see some of the country we had not yet seen. We especially liked *Turrialba* where we stayed at a beautiful inn called *Casa Turire*, a plantation owned and operated by Costa Ricans.

In 1999, Jason moved to the *Osa Peninsula* where he is managing a property and doing sailing charters to observe dolphins and whales. We still have only seen one quarter of this intriguing country and look forward to many more expeditions.

What To Pack

Remember that it is very hot and humid on the Pacific coast – only 9 degrees north of the Equator. Shorts, T-shirts, bathing suits, beach towels, flip-flops for walking on the beach which gets so hot you will burn your feet, mosquito repellent, sun block (at least 30), binoculars, medication against stomach upsets, etc., and a camera are recommended. Long-sleeved shirts, long pants and running shoes or hiking boots are recommended for rain forest or jungle trips – avoid short shorts, tank tops and flimsy footwear on jungle treks!

Surprisingly, annoying bugs and insects are not quite the problem we thought they would be. However, in Guanacaste province, a small outbreak of dengue fever caused by mosquito bites has prompted health officials to warn people travelling in that area to use mosquito repellent with a deet factor of at least 23.

For the Central Valley and the jungles, you need rain gear, umbrella, flashlight, windbreaker and/or sweater for cooler temperatures. Although dress is very informal, it is a good idea to pack one dressy outfit and a jacket for more formal occasions.

Chapter 6
Health Care in Costa Rica

A hush has descended on the Central Valley. Only the songs of birds and the hum and buzz of insects break the silence as they swoop and soar about their business. Even the sugar mill is quiet and the siren calling the men to work is still. The sugar cane fields offer no nightly spectacle of roaring fires. The farmers are at rest. It is *Semana Santa* (Holy Week) in Costa Rica, when everything comes to a grinding halt on Holy Thursday and Good Friday. In the countryside, shops, businesses and restaurants are shut up tight and not even buses run. It is said that in the old days, people did not venture out on these two days for fear of being stoned as punishment for disturbing the tranquillity. These are days for peace and meditation.

From the Posada Mimosa guest book:

The flowers and grounds are beautiful. Thank you for spending so much time on everything.

Rhea, Arkansas

At the other extreme, for the people of San Jose and surroundings, it is an excuse to flock to the beaches and party. Holy Saturday is the day of big celebration. They call it Pre-Resurrection Day. After attending midnight mass, congregations spill out into parks in front of churches and celebrate with fireworks and music. Our story will begin with *Semana Santa* because it signifies the beginning of new life and the passing of the old, and that is how I see our adventure here.

When the Unthinkable Happens

An emergency triple bypass could hardly have been a more inauspicious beginning. You never think it will happen to you, especially if you have never been sick a day in your life. After all, having twice flirted with death – escaping from Communists in former East Germany and surviving the Dresden fire-bombing in World War 2 – you rarely think that illness will strike and certainly not while visiting a foreign country. Naturally, you automatically took all the necessary insurance in case the unthinkable happened, but having travelled the world without worry, you did not give illness a second thought. But strike it did, on May 12, 1993, the second day of our second trip to Costa Rica, a scouting mission to check out the possibilities of living and retiring here.

We had just returned from an evening at the theatre in San Jose, and Martin complained of indigestion from something he had eaten. He also felt clammy and his breathing was restricted. We phoned the front desk (we were staying at the Canadian-owned Grano de Oro) and asked for a doctor. The hotel did not have a doctor on staff, and arranged for us to go to the clinic.

We took a taxi to the *Clinica Biblica* in San Jose, where a doctor greeted us and whisked Martin into an examination room right away – no waiting, no questions asked. The doctor, who had trained at Toronto's Wellesley Hospital, suspected a heart problem, but an ECG and blood tests showed nothing major. Dr. Zamora said he would like to keep Martin in for observation and more tests. They did more tests immediately (it was now midnight), and discovered two arteries were 95% blocked and a third was 87% blocked – he needed an emergency triple bypass! He could not be flown home and he had very little time.

They operated immediately, before we even had time to be nervous. Twelve hours had passed from the time he went into the clinic until the operation. He could have died waiting for a space in a hospital in another country. So when I tell people that all this took place in Costa Rica, they shriek COSTA RICA!, as if it is some sort of Banana Republic. In the next breath they ask "Weren't you nervous?" Not for a moment.

"Pocket Book Medicine"

The doctors, who all spoke excellent English having been trained in the U.S., Canada or Europe, explained every step they were taking, all the details of the heart operation, the prognosis for the future, etc. They were splendid, caring and kind. Dr. Pucci, the country's leading cardiovascular surgeon, even changed Martin's dressing, not often heard of for a surgeon!

Martin had round-the-clock nursing care for two nights, and stayed in a large, private room. We were asked to provide a $500 deposit on our credit card. Compare this to the United States where they practise "pocket book medicine" – if you cannot pay, you are refused care and are moved on to another hospital. Yes, Canadians, there is another country where you can enjoy excellent health care without being bankrupted, although it is changing. The easy part of this whole story was the Costa Rican part. The hardest was when we returned to Canada and started the frustrating battle with OHIP (Ontario Health Insurance Plan) and insurance companies.

See Appendix 1 for the details of the cost of Martin's surgery in Costa Rica.

Insurance

Martin's hospital stay in Costa Rica resulted in an incredibly complicated and difficult time with insurance. Like many people, we never thought it would happen to us, so we never bothered to check what insurance we actually had and what it covered. We blithely travelled the world, confident that all we had to do was dial the "Worldwide Assistance" number most insurance companies provide and all would be taken care of. Instead, we found out that OHIP does not deal with secondary insurers (OHIP is the primary insurer in the case of Ontario residents), nor do they like to talk to Worldwide Assistance. Result: lack of communication and confusion for all. OHIP will pay $400 Canadian a day out of country ONLY for emergency services, and $200 a day for any other medical problem, and OHIP decides if it is an emergency or not.

Dealing With OHIP and Insurance Companies

As soon as Martin entered the clinic, we contacted Worldwide Assistance Services, Inc. (also known as Europe Assistance), the number our personal insurance company told us to contact if we needed medical help while travelling outside the country. They said, "not to worry," they would take care of everything. They were very reassuring, co-operative and helpful – they even paid an advance on the hospital bill. Provincial government health care (OHIP in our case) is the primary insurer and any additional private extended health coverage is secondary (in our case Laurentian Imperial, one of the better companies to deal with, according to Worldwide Assistance). It all sounded simple and straightforward and certainly there was nothing complicated about Martin's bill. We thought the various insurance people would take care of everything. Not so.

After dozens of phone calls, faxes, and correspondence, the final settlement happened eight months after surgery. After trying to sort out the problems, we concluded that OHIP was the source of the difficulties because it refused to communicate with our other insurance company. The client (us) had to take full control of everything. Copies of hospital bills were sent to OHIP at least three times, never to be found because of being sent from office to office.

While OHIP was dragging its feet, our insurance company, Laurentian Imperial, could not pay its share of the bills, as they did not know their share. Laurentian Imperial communicated with us constantly and worked hard at getting things moving.

According to a spokesman at OHIP, normally either the hospital sends the bills to OHIP, or the patient pays up front and then collects from OHIP. OHIP then pays the hospital directly and informs the patient with copies of paid bills, and copies are sent to the personal insurance company who pays the balance. However it did not work this way in our case, and who knows in how many other cases.

Worldwide Assistance Services, Inc. (WAS)

A spokesman for WAS sent me the following fax clarifying the steps Canadians should take to be prepared to handle medical crises – especially the payment of medical invoices – when travelling.

"WAS" is an emergency travel assistance company located in Washington, D.C. and provides services to the

policyholders of numerous Canadian insurance companies. We have over 10 years of experience in dealing with this issue, and have seen many changes in the past two years due to the reductions in out-of-province coverage offered by the various provincial plans.

I think most Canadians know that in order to minimize expenses incurred while outside the home province, they need supplemental insurance provided either through their employer's group policy or through an individual retail policy purchased through a travel agent. If the traveller chooses to use their group insurance, s/he should look into whether that policy offers the following benefits:

1) *Out-of-province (country) medical expenses coverage & its limits.*

2) *Direct payment of medical expenses to the provider to avoid having the traveller pay anything out of his/her own pockets.*

3) *Emergency medical evacuation coverage and its limits.*

4) *A full range of travel assistance services, including cash advances, return of dependent children, pre-trip information, etc.*

By taking this extra step of inquiring into the coverage offered by the policy, the traveller can avoid a lot of hassle should a medical emergency occur. Some Canadian insurers offer to pay the medical provider directly, and will then submit those invoices to the provincial health plan for reimbursement on the policyholder's behalf. This guarantees that the medical provider receives the money quickly, as the provincial governments are not known for their speedy claims processing, and prevents the policyholder from incurring any out-of-pocket expenses while travelling. This procedure of paying up front, then submitting on the traveller's behalf to the provincial plan is normally coordinated through the travel assistance company contracted to provide service on the traveller's insurance policy.

If the insurance company does not offer this benefit, the traveller should see whether the doctor or hospital in question would bill out to the provincial plan and/or the traveller's private insurer. Some foreign medical providers will agree to bill the provincial plans directly, relieving the traveller from having to come up with so much cash to pay the bills. This, however, is not the norm in our experience. Most foreign medical providers are leery of billing foreign insurers, scared that they will never see payment. Providers in Florida, especially, do not like to bill OHIP and the others because of the length of time it takes to receive payment. Therefore, the traveller may have to pay the medical expenses up front, then file a claim first with his/her provincial plan. Once the provincial plan has paid its portion of the medical expenses, the traveller must then submit a claim directly with the insurance company, showing proof that the provincial plan has already paid. This is a lengthy and costly process to the traveller. It would be helpful to know this, however, before anything happens.

A travel assistance company such as ours will be able to give the traveller this information. I strongly encourage all Canadians who are going to be spending an extended period of time abroad to find out which insurance they have, which travel assistance company is connected with that policy, and then to call the assistance number to ask *what procedures are followed when medical expenses are incurred. This phone call will save a lot of headaches dur-*

ing a crisis when the traveller needs to be concentrating on other items.

Your recent experience with the bills from the hospital in Costa Rica is not unusual. We tried to be as helpful as possible in speeding things along, but dealing with the government is never a quick process. Please feel free to contact me at 800-368-7878 should you have any questions and I wish you and your husband a very safe stay in Costa Rica.

Sincerely,

Timothy H. Oneacre
Director of Operations

The Costa Rican Medical Profession

So what does the Costa Rican medical profession think of treating foreigners and not being sure when or if they will be paid? Dr. Hugo Villegas del Carpio, one of the team of doctors who operated on Martin has this to say:

"There is no protection that we will be paid for the services we offer - we trust! We trust the patients and we trust that insurance companies will pay, that it will come through sooner than later. Otherwise the alternative is to treat people like in the U.S. The patient has to sit there until the hospital checks whether he can pay or not. If you can't pay, too bad, go to the next hospital. We can't be like that in Costa Rica. It's not our character; we are caring people. We cannot deny medical care to someone in distress. Sooner or later, things will even out. People over 70 here say things have changed a lot. In the old days, to confirm an obligation you could take a single hair from

91

your head or your beard and give it to the debtor, like you were guaranteeing the debt with a part of your body. This was a solemn promise."

"We have lots of problems with insurance. Nobody seems to know what's happening. Most patients will help us because they know it's such a problem. It usually takes about a year to collect with many faxes back and forth. I remember one man from Texas who had about 12 insurance companies to deal with. Most tourists don't know the procedure to follow. They are just given a phone number with no other information and are under the impression the phone number is the key. Out of 34 emergency open - heart cases in the last two years, about 10 cases have not been paid as yet and they have been mainly from the US. Usually Europeans are able to pay the initial account at the beginning of treatment and during their hospital stay most accounts have been paid. People from Spain are the biggest problem -could be a cultural bias because they think they still own us!"

Medical Options

Dr. Villegas explained the public and private medical options:

"The Costa Rican government does not involve itself with private practice. Everyone, including tourists, is accepted at a public hospital BUT the foreigners' insurance form is not accepted in the public hospitals. The patient has to pay the bill before leaving, if you don't pay, you don't leave. The government will have nothing to do with private

insurance companies. However, the private sector will accept other arrangements."

Medical Insurance

To qualify for insurance while living or travelling in Costa Rica, your legal status is not important. Whether you are a resident, pensioner or tourist you are eligible to apply. If you have been in the country less than a year, you must get a medical certificate from a licensed doctor as well as an AIDS test and urine test. If you have been in the country over a year, you don't need to submit tests – simply contact an agent. Do not attempt to get the insurance yourself; you will need an agent to do the paper work.

There are 2 government medical insurance plans.

**C.C.S.S. –
National Costa Rican socialised medical system:**

- Covers doctors visits, medication, examinations and hospitalization.
- Doctors are assigned to the patient.
- Covers pre-existing medical conditions.
- Covers all medicals, including dental and eye exams.

Reasons to have this plan:

- You have pre-existing health conditions and do not qualify for the INS insurance.
- You take medication on a regular basis.
- Have it as major medical in case of serious illness.

*COST:
Younger than 55 years old, $55 per month.
55 years old or older, $37 per month. (1998 rates)*

Monthly premiums cover all illnesses for the member and his/her immediate family for that month.

INS –
The semi-autonomous government insurance company:

- Covers 80% of the doctor's visits, medication, examinations and hospitalization.

- Individual chooses doctor.

- Does not cover any existing medical condition.

- Does not cover most dental or eye exams, treatments or glasses, preventive medical check-up, illness or disorders related to female reproductive organs dur ing the first twelve months of coverage, or the birth of a baby during the first 6 months of coverage.

Reasons to have this plan:

- You can choose your own doctor.

- You can make doctor appointments with less red tape.

> *COST:*
> *Rates depend on age and sex.*
> *20% deductible is paid for each doctor visit.*

You can be insured up to age 100! There is a discount if more than one person is insured on the same policy. If you take out membership in the American Legion or Residents' Association of Costa Rica (ARCR) you are eligible for their group policy. The policy will also cover medical expenses abroad (you pay the fees and INS reimburses you according to what the costs would have been in Costa Rica). For example, if you have surgery in Canada and it costs $3,000, but would only cost $2,000 in Costa Rica, INS will pay the Costa Rican rate.

N.B.: INS has since refused Martin insurance coverage because of his triple by-pass. They did not notify us of this decision. Martin found out when he phoned his insurance agent to see how things were coming along. Apparently they will not put in writing why they refuse you, nor will they call you to notify you.

To find out the current cost of a policy, contact David Garrett at GARRETT & ASSOCIATES or buy his book Insurance in Costa Rica. TEL: (506) 233-2455; FAX: (506) 222-0007

Plastic Surgery

Dr. Villegas says that planeloads of visitors come from the US to take advantage of the excellent plastic surgery facilities available in Costa Rica. They make a holiday out of it and, after surgery, spend two weeks on the beach recovering, returning home with a new look! Both the highly skilled surgeons and the much lower cost of these services attract these visitors.

See Appendix 2 for examples of costs of plastic surgery in Costa Rica.

Dental Care

Some dentists in Costa Rica are English speaking and offer excellent dental care and cosmetic procedures much cheaper than in North America. They have specialists in prosthodontics (bridges, crowns and implants), root canals, etc. We often have guests at our Posada who have their dental work done here and have a holiday at the same time for less than it would cost in North America.

USTED INGRESA AL PARQUE NACIONAL BAJO SU PROPIO RIESGO.

POÁS VOLCANO IS IN ACTIVITY
YOU ENTER UNDER YOUR OWN RISK
SPN – MIRENEM

Chapter 7
How To Obtain Residency

You have visited Costa Rica a few times, you like what you see, and you are now ready to think about residency options. Thoroughly think through your reasons for living, investing or retiring in Costa Rica. The following are the categories for temporary residency status. After 3-5 years, you may apply for permanent status. Pensionados, rentistas and inversionistas can claim their spouses and children under 18 as dependents. A child between 18 and 25 can be a dependent if he/she is enrolled in a university.

From the Posada Mimosa guest book:

This was the children's first time to your wonderful country. You gave us many exciting adventures!!!

John & Leslie, California

Rick and Marge:

My advice to people who want to move to Costa Rica? Don't move to Costa Rica unless you are the type of person who has decided that it's o.k. to take risks, that you have some financial safe situation in the country in which you reside. I certainly would not recommend coming here if your financial situation is paltry or if you don't have a definite way to make a living.

Pensionado

You must be retired with a pension of at least US600 (or equivalent) a month from a qualified retirement plan or pension source, such as a government pension. The qualifying income must be for the applicant only – combined income is usually acceptable. The $600 must be deposited in colones in a Costa Rican bank every month. You must live in Costa Rica at least four months every year.

Rentista

You must have investments, such as a certificate of deposit or annuity, that generate at least $1,000 US a month (12,000 US per year) for five years, and it must be changed into colones. Investments must come from the same source and not from a combination of sources. Rentistas must live in the country at least 6 months every year.

An approved financial institution (in a foreign country or in Costa Rica) must guarantee in writing that:

- They hold sufficient funds in a stable and permanent account to provide an income of at least $US1,000 per month for at least five years.

- If the financial conditions above change, the financial institution agrees to notify the *Instituto Costarricense de Turismo (ICT)*.

- The monthly income will be sent to the rentista in Costa Rica.

- Qualifying funds are in the name of the applicant.

Form letters for the above conditions are available to members from the Association of Residents of Costa Rica. Approved banks in Costa Rica, for a deposit of $US 60,000 will satisfy all government requirements for this status of residency. Deposits in state owned banks are government guaranteed without limit.

As a RENTISTA, you must prove your continuing income every five years.

Other Requirements for Pensionados and Rentistas

- Income must be changed into colones at a government bank or an approved private bank in Costa Rica.

  PENSIONADO: $7,200 US per year

  RENTISTA: $12,000 US per year

- You must renew your identification card *(carnet)* every two years. The government of Costa Rica charges a $100 US tax for each renewed identification card.

- You and your dependents cannot earn a salary or sup plant a Costa Rican in a work situation.

- You can own and operate a business and pay yourself, and/or make investments.

Inversionista

This means investor status, and it is granted to people who invest at least $50,000 in special projects like tourism or exports, $100,000 in a reforestation project and $200,000 in any other business in Costa Rica. An instant way to get residency is to pay $50,000 as an investment in a teak corporation, but who knows when you will receive a return, if any, on your investment. Another alternative is to buy a home or make an approved invest- ment of $40,000 or more, plus pay another $10,000 non- refundable to be used for low cost housing. You must visit Costa Rica at least once a year.

Permanent Residency Status

After two years of PENSIONADO, RENTISTA OR INVER- SIONISTA status, application can be made for permanent residency. This is usually unrestricted, and working is permitted. Citizens of Spain can apply for permanent residency right away.

Permanent residents must visit Costa Rica at least once a year. $300 US must be deposited with the Government of Costa Rica as a guarantee.

First Degree Relative Status

If you have parents, siblings, spouses or children who are Costa Rican residents, you are eligible for residency, but you still must apply for it. You are also eligible if you marry a resident of Costa Rica.

The Quickest and Cheapest Way

According to the *Association of Residents of Costa Rica*, pensionado-rentista status takes only 4-6 months to acquire and is the quickest and cheapest way to become a temporary resident. Until April 1992, pensioners and foreigners with guaranteed incomes could import $7,000 worth of their household goods and one car into the country duty-free. Now pensionados and rentistas must pay import taxes of up to 100 percent on the things they want to bring into the country.

Pensionados, rentistas and investors can own their own businesses, but they cannot legally work for someone else. In the past, if you did not want to be bothered with the hassle of getting residency, Canadians, Americans and most Europeans were allowed to stay in the country for 90 days. After three months, they had to leave the country for at least 72 hours. Upon their return, they could get another entry stamp good for another three months. If they overstayed their 90 days, they could buy an exit visa for a small fee. Otherwise, they paid a fine at immigration as they left the country.

All that changed in 1996, when the government decreed that all foreigners who live in Costa Rica must file for legal residency or face deportation – being a "perpetual tourist" is no longer possible. However, enforcing these laws is difficult since potential residents are faced with incredibly slow, inefficient and frustrating bureaucracy.

> *To save you the headaches and for more information and help in becoming a resident, contact the Association of Residents of Costa Rica: Casa Canada, Ave. 4 &St. 40, San Jose, Costa Rica, 200 m. south of the Paseo Colon. Tel: 233-8068 or 221-2053, fax 233-1152. The mailing address is P.O. Box 232-1007, Centro Colon, San Jose, Costa Rica, or Remarsa/ARCR #1919, P.O. Box 025292, Miami, Fl. 33102-5292 E-Mail: arcrsacc@sol.racsa.co.cr; Web Site: http//www.amerispan.com/arcr*

How To Apply for Residency

We were confused when we first started the process, and began by considering investor status in August 1993. We were told it would take a few weeks to four months. When we visited again in November, our lawyer advised us to switch to rentista status because it is less complicated. In the end, after three years, we eventually changed to family status, thanks to our son who got residency status under an amnesty. At first the procedure sounds simple enough, but it involves a lot of paper work, bureaucracy and an incredible amount of patience and fortitude!

Here are the things you have to do:

- Find yourself a good lawyer – do NOT attempt to file the application yourself if you value your sanity! In Costa Rica, a good, reliable lawyer is an absolute MUST.

- Open a bank account in US dollars. Eventually you must also have a "colones" account. To do this you need two references from people who already have bank accounts in your chosen bank.

Documents Needed (in the case of Canadians)

- A notarized medical letter from your doctor declaring you to have had a recent physical check-up, HIV tests, blood tests and that you are free of communicable diseases.

- Notarized marriage certificates (if applicable) for you and your spouse.

- Notarized birth certificate for applicant, spouse and dependent children.

- Photocopies of all the used pages of your passport.

- Royal Canadian Mounted Police clearance or other police clearances from last place of Residency.

- 8 front and 2 side photographs.

- Take these documents to the Official Documents Services of the Government of Ontario (Ontario residents), Main Floor, 724 Bay Street, Toronto, Ont. M5G 1N5 and have them notarized, (it cost us $51).

- Take the notarized documents to your local Costa Rican consulate to be translated into Spanish and stamped. Include $200 payable to your local consulate that covers the cost of application.

- When everything is assembled, send it to your lawyer in Costa Rica or send it through the consulate.

If you are applying for pensionada or rentista status, you also have to obtain a notarized letter from your accountant or other financial officer to prove you will have the required income. We also had to be fingerprinted. When we switched to the family category, we had to submit notarized documents detailing our investment here. During this whole process, be prepared to wait endlessly.

We finally received our residency "*cedula*" in June 1996, three and a half years after we first applied, a very small booklet which entitles you to work in Costa Rica, live here indefinitely, and pay more airport exit taxes. You are also obliged to get a Costa Rican driving licence within ten days of acquiring residency (I still have not done this) and then you have to renew the "cedula" every year. I lost my "cedula" on my first trip out of the country and just got a second one after a three-month wait!

John and Mary:

"I think if anybody wants to make a permanent move, they need to stay at least a year and think about it and see the whole system. All we need to do is look at the school where our kids go to see how many families just get frustrated and move back. They just throw up their hands and say "to hell with it."

Our daughter, Louise, said to us a couple of years ago when we had just moved here "What would anybody who had only lived within a really structured lifestyle in Canada or the United States do here?" You can't live within a structured lifestyle - you have to live according to what happens that day and you have to adjust to it. Unless you can be flexible and unless you can put up with the frustrations and live with them, you're not going to make it in this country, it's just not possible."

Chapter 8
Setting Up a Business

Learning Spanish

In preparation for our eventual move to Costa Rica, we decided to plunge into Spanish courses. We spent a month at Conversa in Santa Ana, 15 minutes outside San Jose, though it feels far from the rush and noise of the city. The view is one of the most spectacular in this valley: butterflies and birds dart in and out, and the occasional cow comes to pay a visit! It is a bucolic scene with nature providing a backdrop of never-ending variety - blazing sunshine one minute, banished by a sudden rainstorm, crowned with a rainbow sunset. We stayed at La Casona, a two-storey building with simple, comfortable rooms, each with its own bathroom. There is a common sitting area and a kitchen. The school also places students in host families, if they prefer.

From the Posada Mimosa guest book:

We travelled around the country and stayed at many hotels and B&B's.
Posada Mimosa is by far the Best!
You definitely get our vote.

Norma & David,
Toronto, Canada

The School

We first met David Kaufman seven years ago. He started *Conversa* in San Jose over 20 years ago and bought his farm in Santa Ana so that students from other countries would have somewhere to stay. David first came to Costa Rica with the US Peace Corps, married a Costa Rican and decided to make his life here.

People of all ages and walks of life study here. When we were there, there was a Swiss diplomat with the Swiss Development Corporation, his Czech-born wife and two teenagers who were on their way to a posting in Bolivia after spending 10 years in Africa; two young American couples in their 30's who decided to take a year out of their lives as a minister, environmentalist and banker, to travel; a German-born Canadian who was about to celebrate her 72nd birthday and was engaged to a Mexican! There was also a lawyer from Miami; a middle-aged couple from California who had just finished hot-air ballooning over the rain forests of Costa Rica, white-water rafting and rock climbing; a young German chemical engineer; an American fireman from Idaho who sold up everything to move down here on his first ever visit; and Christie from Guelph, Ontario whom I met through our newsletter.

The classes were very demanding but excellent. No sooner did we arrive than we had to write a test. We were rank beginners – I scored 33 out of a 100 and Martin 22! We could only go up from there! Our teacher was lively and enthusiastic, the eldest of 12 children. Each week we had a different teacher and there was homework every night. It was a lot of fun and the days passed quickly. Summer was just starting, meaning the beginning of the dry season.

After three weeks, Martin and I decided to postpone our last week until later because we had to spend time looking for real estate. We had learnt a fair amount of Spanish, but had a few reservations about the course. Looking at it as a language teacher, I found the teaching methods dated since they were based on the Peace Corps model of the 60's and 70's. The course was very grammar-based – pages of 130 irregular verbs. If you are a grammar nut, do not mind the different teachers each week (most of the students did not like it), and want to spend your entire time studying, this course is ideal. *Conversa* is considered to be one of the best schools in Costa Rica.

Learning Spanish was only one of our goals for this trip, and it should have been the only goal. To get the most out of the course, one should devote all one's attention to it. Perhaps we attempted to do too much. Nevertheless, we are now able to communicate with Costa Ricans in their own language, which is a "must." Once off the tourist track and living in the countryside as we do, there is very little English spoken.

Setting Up a Company

Rick and Marge:

"With our Costa Rican experience, we did all the wrong things at all the wrong times, yet we had done it and there was no turning back. From that point on, we tried everything that was suggested to us. We had plenty of people with plenty of suggestions. Most of them were incorrect. Our biggest downfall at first was no kind of business leadership. Nobody who knew about dealing with tour companies and tourism. It is a clickish kind of business, very political. I found that tourism has nothing to do with quality or special, unique situations, events or locations that people might want to see. It has to do with money, it has to do with whom you pay off, whom you know, how long you have been in a certain place. If a tour company has a destination, whether it's mediocre or not, if they are making money, they don't want to rock the boat, they will do it for the next 30 years as long as they make a big profit."

The most important thing to do first is find a lawyer. You need a lawyer for practically everything. We inquired at the Costa Rican consulate in Toronto, and they gave us the name of the firm *Faccio & Canas*. When Martin was in hospital after his bypass operation, one of the principals of the firm visited him and said that what we needed were young, energetic lawyers, and suggested Adrian Alvarenga Odio of the firm *Bufete, Weisleder and Odio*. Adrian's aunt was the only female judge on the International Tribunal looking into war crimes in the former Yugoslavia and is now a vice-president in the government in charge of the environment. His mother has spent a long time in the Costa Rican diplomatic service. He also speaks English and French. Adrian's partner and cousin, Sergio Sanchez, has helped us set up our company, helped us open bank accounts, buy real estate and seek residency status, guided us through our bad experience with a Canadian builder, registered our cars, helped Martin with registering an organic agricultural product he is importing, and generally helped us with endless paperwork. Honest they are, and energetic too!

Although foreigners are not allowed to work in Costa Rica until they have residency, they can own any kind of business they want. Foreigners who want to own a business should establish a company. The most recommended one is a *Sociedad Anonima* (S.A.) that, once registered, can engage in any type of business. Many foreigners opt for tourism, such as bed and breakfasts, tour companies, language schools, consulting businesses and import-export companies. The scope is limitless, and the most successful people are entrepreneurial risk-takers who have sufficient capital to back them up. It is difficult, if not impossible, to get bank loans and mortgages, and they can be very expensive if you do manage to get them. There are many success stories but many more failures, mostly because everything here takes twice as long and costs twice as much as one thinks. Too many people come here under-capitalized, immediately find themselves in trouble and watch their dreams (and money) evaporate into thin air. It is wiser to have a stable source of income (e.g. pensions or other savings) if you want to start your own business in Costa Rica.

The key here is:

CAUTION, DO NOT JUMP AT THE FIRST OPPORTUNITY, DO YOUR HOMEWORK, AND LOOK BEFORE YOU LEAP!

Once you have a company duly registered with a "*cedula*" (similar to a social security number), you can use it to open bank accounts in US dollars and Costa Rican colones. Keep most of your money in dollars and only change it into colones as you need it, because the colon is devaluing about 20% every year against the dollar.

John and Mary

"From a business perspective, I think when people come here they look and see that the country needs this, the country needs that, using the United States and Canada as reference points based on their experience there. A lot of the things you see work up there can't work here because the money is not available, people don't have the income. So maybe it will work in twenty years but now it doesn't. A lot of people come and do the tourist circuit where everything is beautiful and they don't see the garbage in the rivers, they don't see the poverty. They just go to the really nice tourist hotels and see the beautiful parks and beaches. So they leave with a really good feeling about Costa Rica but that's not the reality of the country. Likewise, when you go through that whole circuit, you can see what the country needs from a business perspective. Actually, everything that I have analyzed over the last five years, somebody is doing already."

Banking

The first time we set foot in a bank was a pretty daunting experience. It was on one of our first trips, we had limited knowledge of Spanish, and thank goodness we had our lawyers with us. They immediately steered us to an account executive on the 6th floor of the Banco Anglo de Costa Rica, to avoid the endless lines of patiently waiting people. Anybody doing business in Costa Rica usually has a "gofer" do all their banking, and businessmen have account executives looking after their transactions.

On one of our visits, we had a good look at the banking system through first hand experience. In a rush we exchanged Dollars at the *Banco de Costa Rica* at the airport, the teller did not give us a proper receipt and cheated us out of $300. When we discovered the discrepancy we reported the incident to the main branch of *Banco de Costa Rica* in San Jose and, with the help of one of our teachers, reported our problem to the head of the security and investigative unit of the bank. We must have had at least six detectives asking us our story! They did their utmost to trace the problem and ended up tracking down the guilty employee, firing him and giving us the $300 owing us – all done in the space of a week! Our thanks went out to security chief Willie Bianchini and his team who were so helpful and co-operative. Their parting words to us, "never trust anybody!" came back to haunt us many times. If you find yourself short-changed, by all means report it.

CHECK AND DOUBLE-CHECK ALL FINANCIAL TRANSACTIONS YOU MAKE AND KNOW THE EXCHANGE RATE.

To open a bank account, you need the recommendations of two people who do business with the bank. By now, we had our company "cedula" which was needed for all the paperwork and, of course, our passports. We opened a US dollar account and a colones account in the Banco Anglo de Costa Rica. We had to deposit a minimum balance in both accounts and could not write a cheque against the accounts for 7 days. Unlike Canada, where you can do all your business with the same teller, in Costa Rica we had to go to yet another department to order our chequebooks, which were ready in a couple of days.

Little did we know that almost a year later, this venerable bank would go into bankruptcy, resulting in the biggest banking crisis in the country's history! Our lawyer had alerted us to the possibility of the bank's demise, so we had very little in our accounts, which was transferred very easily into our new accounts at the *Banco Nacional*, after going through all the paper work again. To the government's credit, it honoured its guarantee of deposits, so depositors were not on the losing end.

The government guarantees and insures deposits in the three remaining state-run banks – the *Banco Nacional*, the *Banco de Costa Rica* and *Banco Credito Agricola* de Cartago. However, the many private banks do not enjoy these same guarantees. *The Canadian Scotia Bank* recently merged with a local private bank.

It takes at least 8 days to transfer money from an account in Canada. We have found that the best (although expensive) way to get instant money is to use a credit card. All the major credit cards are honoured here with little or no hassle. There are also bank machines in some banks, however they do not always work. It is almost impossible for foreigners to get loans at state-owned banks. Theoretically, credit is available in stores, but their interest rates are ridiculous. Ensuring one has enough cash on hand is a constant challenge.

One last point: avoid banking on Mondays, Fridays or the day before a holiday! We used to get terribly impatient waiting endlessly in lines, but now we have adjusted our expectations and tell ourselves it will be at least an hour and sometimes are pleasantly surprised when it is less. When we first moved to Costa Rica, our local bank in Grecia had line-ups for people with colones accounts and line-ups for the dollar accounts and for exchange of travellers' cheques. We had comfortable chairs to sit in as we waited, and there was usually a self-appointed "policeman" to control the traffic and tell everybody who was next up as we shuffled from chair to chair – a bit like musical chairs! Nobody ever jumped the queue – Costa Ricans are unfailingly polite when it comes to waiting. It was interesting people-watching and was a social occasion for most Ticos, as they chattered to acquaintances, clapping shoulders, kissing cheeks and shaking hands. We also met other foreigners and passed the time finding out what they were doing and where they were going. As of 1997, our bank changed this procedure, and everybody now lines up in the same queue. We now have our "gofer," and we rarely set foot in a bank.

John and Mary:

"If you don't have personal wealth, you have to have resources outside the country to draw from, whether it be business partners or whatever. Without that, you can't make it work. You need to have the ability to live through the frustrations daily and hourly. I'm doing business in a new environment where I don't know the culture, I don't know the language and I don't know basically how business is done. So you need two things. You need to be able to cope with all the frustrations and get through them and you need the financial backing to sustain yourself until your business gets on its feet and you can make a living from what you generate."

Chapter 9
All About Real Estate

If you have visited Costa Rica at least four times, found a lawyer, formed a company, and decided that this country is for you, the next step is to buy real estate.

The Bureaucratic Process

Before actually buying real estate, make sure to follow these steps:

1. Visit Costa Rica several times at different times of the year to make sure that this country is really for you.

2. Once you have decided that you would like to live here, find a reputable lawyer and form a company. You will then receive a "*cedula juridica,*" which acts as proof of corporation registration.

3. Decide on a residency status and get your papers together. No matter what you are told, count on this process taking a year or two. All our papers were in order and our lawyer had sent them to the appropriate office, when we found out our RCMP clearance had become stale-dated and that, if we did not get a new clearance in 5 days, the whole application would be cancelled! Recently, some body who had been waiting for pensionado status for three years complained to the Ombudsman, who intervened, and within a week he received it.

4. Keep every single piece of paper you are given and do not let any paper out of your hands without making copies.

From the Posada Mimosa guest book:

Although it has been said many times, many ways, you both are truly one of a kind. Just your presence makes this a lovely place to be. Your hospitality is the kind spoken of in the Bible at Matthew 25:35: "I was a stranger and you received me hospitably".

Julie, Longmont, Colorado

Buying Real Estate

Ownership of real estate in Costa Rica is fully guaranteed by the constitution to all, including foreigners. Compulsory real estate licensing of brokers does not exist in Costa Rica, consequently everybody and his brother can act as sales agents. Our experience has been that very few are helpful.

How did we buy our property?

First we established the criteria for what we wanted.

1. Where – beach or Central Valley? We decided on the Central Valley rather than the beach (even though we love the ocean) because we feel there is more to do and the climate is more agreeable. If we want to visit the beaches, it only takes us 1 hour and 20 minutes to go there.

2. Where in the Central Valley? We really were not sure, so we let climate be our guide. We decided on Santa Ana, Ciudad Colon, Alajuela, Heredia or Grecia

3. Proximity to the airport.

4. Country rather than city.

5. Acreage so we could build.

6. An existing house with a telephone and the other infrastructure. (The telephone is extremely important as it can take as long as two years to get one.)

7. A spectacular view.

8. Price range.

115

Quite a tall order!

I first started looking for property in May 1993 when Martin was in the hospital and the market was at its peak. It is not as common in Costa Rica to use real estate agents as it is in North America, but I had no idea where to start, so I opted for an agent. The first agent I had was an American woman who had lived in Costa Rica for twenty years and was full of useful information. She drove me around the different areas and I liked two of the first houses she showed me. One was in *Ciudad Colon* and the other in La Garita, complete with furniture, satellite dish, telephones, fax machines, etc. I did not think it was prudent to buy the first house I saw, so we returned to Canada better informed but not quite ready to buy. The wise buyer will take time and we recommend several visits before actually deciding.

We returned again in August and I tried to contact the first agent but she never returned my calls. Instead we chose *Coronado Realty* out of the *Tico Times* because it was British and Costa Rican managed. Barry Ashworth was British and Xavier Barquero was Tico, and we found it very helpful to have both perspectives in our search for real estate. We continued looking in *Atenas* and *Alajuela*, but found nothing. We returned once more in November, and went to see a property near Grecia we were supposed to have seen on a former visit. Barry kept saying it was a bit of a dump and needed work, but it seemed to have the potential for what we wanted to do. We loved it instantly, and put in an offer that was accepted by the American owners who were moving to Lake Arenal.

Offer to Purchase

An offer to purchase in Costa Rica is not at all like it is in North America. At the beginning of December, we simply faxed a letter with our offer. Our lawyer prepared an Option to Buy that became legally binding upon a deposit of $10,000 made in trust to our lawyer. The rest of the work is up to the lawyer who checks the following:

1. Copies of vendor's Title Registration, proof of clear title. See if old charges against the property are elimi nated (no liens, old mortgages, etc.). Obtain a copy of the Official Survey Plan. Have all these documents at closing. There can be real problems with title and the same house has been known to be sold twice!

2. Obtain an opinion from an earthquake engineer as to the geological history of the location.

3. Check if the property is affected in any way by being near a national reserve or other existing restrictions.

4. Can we build a swimming pool and casitas using our own septic sewage treatment system? Can we drill water wells? Can we get written proof from the municipality that all this is possible?

5. Copy of existing Bed & Breakfast licence.

6. Telephone to be transferred to us.

We went back to Costa Rica in February 1994 and closed February 21 with no problems, all our questions satisfactorily addressed. Present at the closing were our lawyer, the vendor's lawyer and our real estate agents. Once we handed over our cheque, we were given the keys and our lawyer immediately went to the title office to register title and gave us a copy of the registration.

Although it takes two months to have it officially entered into the system, the contract signed at the lawyers is legally binding. It is very, very important to get this piece of paper, as people have been known to sell the same house to different people in very short order! The vendor also had to sign another legal paper transferring ownership of the telephone to us.

Closing Costs

Closing costs are shared between buyer and seller as follows:

- Real Estate Transfer Tax.
- Registration Fee: .5 percent of sale price.
- Documentary Stamps: .5 percent of sale price.
- Notary Fees: 1.5 percent of the first 1 million colones ($5,000), and 1.25 percent of the balance.
- Mortgage Registration Fees: vary in cost.

The vendors were very helpful and left us a file with all their B & B information, as well as the names of trades people, bankers, lawyers, etc. in the community. We were also invited to a "farewell and welcome" party given by a couple of American neighbours and we met a lot of local Ticos – a great introduction for us. In 1994, most real estate purchases were all cash transactions because the interest rates on mortgages ranged anywhere between 20% and 30% due to high inflation. The current interest rate (2000) on a US mortgage is 13% at Scotia Bank.

John and Mary

I was mainly interested in land development when we came here and we looked everywhere in the country. I looked at land at the beach because that's the first thing everybody wants to do – get a piece of "paradise"at Guanacaste, get a little hotel or bar and live happily every after. But the reality is that it's too isolated and too hot out there.

Most people can spend a week there and love it but if they had to live there year-round, they'd hate it. When you look at the land values, they are so inflated compared to the Central Valley so we chose to start buying property around Grecia which was more reasonable.

What's Hot?

Since we bought at the peak in 1994, the market has changed significantly. 1995 was a slow year due to a downturn in tourism, but things picked up in 1996. Beach prices are prohibitive, so buyers are looking for good buys in the Central Valley. It looks as if the market is moving west of San Jose due to an urban exodus.

So what are the hottest spots? According to an article in the *Tico Times*, the eight most popular areas for buyers are:

- *Alajuela*: Costa Rica's second largest city. Home prices listed between $18,000 - $300,000; land starting at $5 per square meter; rentals from $200 - $2,000 per month. My opinion: too close to the air port and too industrial.

- *Cariari*: Home prices from $100,000 - 500,000, land starting at $50 per square meter; rentals from $700 - $3,000 per month. My opinion: very North American and insulated, similar to a gated community in the United States.

- *Escazu*: Homes listed from $80,000 - 500,000; land prices vary greatly, from $10 - 125 per square meter; rentals from $400 - 3,000 per month. My opinion: over-rated, with lots of crime, noise and traffic.

- *La Garita/Atenas/Orotina*: Homes from $25,000 - 500,000; land from $2-10 per square meter. Rent from $200- 1,500. My opinion: attractive areas and best climate, noted for landscapers and nurseries (viveros). At the time of writing, we hear that Taiwanese are buying up choice fincas.

- *Sabana/Rohrmoser*: Homes between $75,000 - $500,000; land starting at $60 per square meter; rentals from $300-$2,000 per month. Mostly for the embassy crowd and upper class Tico. My opinion: Good, but no comparison to classy neighbourhoods in Canada; noisy and crime-prone.

- *San Pedro/Los Yoses*: To quote the *Tico Times* – " Practically in the city, with close access to the University of Costa Rica and numerous language schools, these areas will become the principal resi dential/commercial/study centre in eastern San Jose." Homes range from $90,000 - $500,000; land from $70-90 per square metre; rentals from $200 (stu dents) to $2,500 per month.

My opinion: I have never been there, so I cannot judge.

- *San Rafael de Heredia*: A mix of modest middle-class Tico homes and mid to upscale residences. Homes between $50 - 500,000; land from $10-35 per square meter; rentals between $200- 1,500. My opinion: Heredia is one of the nicer areas, but be prepared for cooler temperatures and more rainfall. If you are looking for a tropical climate, this is not it.

- *Santa Ana/Ciudad Colon*: Mid to upscale homes from $60,000-$500,000; land starts at $12 per square meter; rentals from $200-1,500 per month. My opinion: This is the area we chose when we first started looking for property. It is still a great area but Santa Ana has an ongoing problem with the tentative designation of the new Central Valley garbage dump being placed on its doorstep.

Note that the towns of Grecia *and* Sarchi *have not hit the top eight. Our area of Costa Rica is the best-kept secret in town, and we're hoping it stays that way! Everybody who stays at our bed and breakfast says this is by far and away the most beautiful area in Costa Rica.*

Grecia and Surroundings

Although *Grecia* is not yet ranked as one of the central valley "hot spots," it has all of the advantages of the current most popular places to live without the escalating real estate costs, high-rise condominiums, hustle and bustle of traffic and too many people. In fact, it has earned the title of "cleanest town" in Latin America and it certainly lives up to its reputation.

Grecia is actually in the municipality of *Alajeula* and is ideally suited for day trips to volcanoes, *Sarchi, Zarcero*, cloud forests etc. It is the pineapple capital of Costa Rica and is dominated by its famous dark red, all-metal church that was shipped from Belgium in the middle 1800's. The surrounding landscape is dream like: rolling farm country dotted with little villages, coffee plantations and sugar cane fields. It has remained unspoilt by the march of progress which is fast overtaking Costa Rica.

We have lived six years now in a small village called *Rincon de Salas*, about 15 minutes from *Grecia*. We picked this area to settle because we like the tranquility of life here, the friendly Tico neighbours and the easy accessibility to other places via the Inter-American Highway. As well, *Grecia* is a transportation hub where buses depart and arrive from destinations all over Costa Rica. All our neighbours are Ticos except for our American friends, Ruth Dixon and Norma Wikler, who live close by. We have to speak Spanish most of the time, and have made some good friends in the community.

We definitely feel very much a part of life here and very much at home. We probably would never have made Tico friends if we were living in an "expat" enclave. They help us with making the right contacts in government and bureaucracies and have helped so much in smoothing the path for us.

Nearby *Sarchi* is famous for its colourful, traditional ox-cart designs derived from Moorish influences, and production of hand-made furniture made of tropical hardwoods. Originally, each district in Costa Rica had its own special design and you could tell by looking at the cart where the driver lived. As late as 1960, the oxcart was the most typical mode of transportation and the only vehicle that could negotiate Costa Rica's rugged terrain. Even today, you frequently see the oxcart drawn by Brahmin oxen doing heavy work.

The father of the former president, Oscar Arias Sanchez made his original fortune hauling coffee by ox-cart to *Puntarenas*. *Zarcero* is further up in the highlands and is famous for its unique Central Park where, for over two decades, Evangelisto Blanco, the park gardener, has been clipping and shaping cypress bushes and hedges into all kinds of exotic animals. He works alone seven days a week including holidays. We had the good luck to watch him at work on one of our visits.

Beach Versus Central Valley

According to Barry Ashworth of Coronado Realty, beach prices are out of sight for most people, but there are still beach properties available in less-developed areas. Hot areas such as *Playas Flamingo, Jaco, Manuel Antonio* and *Tamarindo* are in the "very high" price category, with beachfront properties going for $100-200 a meter. Other "hot" areas include Playas Potrero, Coco and Conchal, on the *Nicoya Peninsula.* Less developed areas where prices are much lower are in the Central Pacific between *Playas Jaco* and *Manuel Antonio* and more remote areas on the *Nicoya Peninsula.*

Unfortunately, there is a widespread perception of Costa Rica as a "cheap" place to live, thanks to overly enthusiastic guide and retirement books. One realtor says that most US customers buying here come from pricier areas of the country, mainly the California coast, plus Germans, Swiss and Italians, who find it relatively cheap to live here compared to Europe.

Real Estate Do-Nots

1. Do not leave your common sense in your home coun try. The basic principles are the same anywhere.
2. Do not put money down without first checking with a recommended broker or lawyer.

3. Do not talk seriously to people in bars about your business.

4. Do not believe in any miracle growth and gross exag gerations.

5. Do not buy into your dreams without first stopping to consider the practicalities involved.

6. Do not necessarily trust people who come from the same country, province or town as you. Check things out thoroughly first.

7. Do not necessarily tacitly accept the recommenda tions of lawyers, brokers, receptionists, bell-boys, barmen and taxi drivers. You need well-referred advice.

8. Do not believe implicitly the ads you read about Real Estate and Investment Opportunities. Consult a pro fessional.

9. Do not believe in projected infrastructure.

10. Do not leave property alone.

11. Do not accept figures as true. You have to do your own assessment with professional help.

The gospel according to Barry Ashworth,
President of Coronado Realty, S.A.
Tel: 011-506-221-31-74, 391-20-80; fax: 223-46-18.

Tips On Getting a Good Price

Whether we like it or not, very often the sight of a foreign buyer sends prices sky-high. Generally speaking, prices fluctuate wildly. Here are some tips to help you get a good price:

124

1. Send a Tico friend on scouting missions to check out areas and prices.

2. To avoid paying high transfer and property taxes, the "real" sales prices of properties are not listed in the National Registry. To determine if the house you are interested in is reasonably priced, check out the area and ask around to see what other properties were sold for.

3. You rarely see "house for sale" signs on Tico proper ties because, very often, their properties have been in the family for generations. However, one never knows when they might be interested in selling. The best thing is to go to the local "pulperia" (small grocery store), and ask around to see if there is anything for sale.

4. Ticos love to haggle. As a result, one is never sure if they really want to sell, or if they are playing a game. Their idea of an entertaining weekend is to take the whole family to look at properties with absolutely no intention of buying! The best bet is to buy from anoth er foreigner to ensure the process does not take too long. If you are selling, be sure to qualify serious buy ers, otherwise you will waste time with "sightseers."

5. Always use a reputable lawyer to close the transac tion.

To Build Or Not To Build

If you decide to build rather than buy an existing home, allow at least a year for the actual construction. Before actually buying the land, do a preliminary study to ensure the land has access to water, drainage, electricity and telephone services. Find out if there are any restrictions on land use. Even though zoning is nonexistent, permits are still required, and it takes time to get them. In fact, some people start to build (including us) before getting the necessary permits. But beware, you will be fined for building without a permit. To get the permit, an architect or civil engineer makes the application for you at the Permit Reception Office. You must also file with the municipality where the house will be built.

Building Permits

To request a building permit, you will need:

- Four copies of construction plans.

- Four copies of surveyor's plans.

- Two copies of property deed.

- One copy of the architect or engineer's consulting contract.

- Approval from the Water and Sewer Institute (AyA) and the Electricity Institute (ICE).

In our case, even though we decided against building from scratch, we did build one "casita"(guest house) and fixed up the existing house. We decided the hassle of building new infrastructure and finding engineers, architects, etc., would be too costly and time-consuming for absentee owners – we wanted to move into something ready-made.

The prudent approach to hiring a potential contractor is to get at least three written quotes that include design, engineering and inspection fees. The contractor provides an agreement document outlining all costs, services and responsibilities, drawn up by his lawyer. The next phase is architecture and engineering, which usually takes about six weeks but will vary according to each project. After approval of the design, the plans are submitted for permitting approvals to the Association of Architects and Engineers, the municipality, and, for tourist-oriented developments, the Tourism Board (ICT). According to our contract, construction should have been completed by September 15, 1994, and we were planning to be open for business by December 1994. Unfortunately, this turned out to be a dream!

Our Building Nightmare

Then began our nightmare. We made a number of mistakes during the planning and construction process. We hope to help you avoid repeating them!

Choosing a Contractor:

We chose the first contractor we met, solely based on the fact that they were Canadians and therefore could speak English and could be trusted. They had excellent letters of reference from the Canadian Embassy. They said they could build us prefab houses at very reasonable costs, and would also build the pool, the rancho and oversee the fixing up of the main house.

Lawyers:

Their lawyer drew up the contract, and we neglected to have our lawyer go over it (unforgivable). We were so anxious to begin construction that our common sense flew out the window! **Always, always** consult your lawyer regarding contracts.

Money Issues:

We gave our contractors too much money up front. We later found out they were using our money for other projects and our workers complained they never had needed materials. They would often be unable to work because nobody could find the contractors (who rarely visited the worksite!). Think twice or even three times before parting with your money.

When our contractors said they had run out of funds, we sent them more money. We subsequently learned that this was a recurring pattern for their projects. They had little idea how to manage, and simply did not deliver. We have heard from other Canadians who ran into trouble with them. At the end of 1996 our contractors went bankrupt. We obtained a fully documented legal and judicial agreement that they were to repay us US $60,000 plus interest, legal fees, etc. They refused to pay, even after signing a document saying they would. We seized their crane, and finally sold it after two years for $25,000, leaving $35,000 still owing. Our lawyers say they should be tried under the criminal code, but that can take up to five years. It took us 3 years to go the civil route. We found there is little effective protection from the law. Remember this when you make contracts and use caution. There is also little protection here for the business person or private individual in connection with labour – everything is in favour of the worker. We tried to get help from the Canadian embassy, but they do not interfere in private cases, even though Canadian funds went to the same Canadian contractors to build low-cost housing here.

Beware of cost over-runs. Put into your contract that you want work finished by a certain date at a certain cost. If work is not concluded on time, put in a penalty clause. Also, include a bonus clause if the work is finished before the due date. ***Pay only for work that is completed.***

If you hire an architect and contractor, make sure they give you receipts and an accounting for every dollar spent, and check them carefully. The person who receives merchandise should sign every invoice. In Costa Rica, the law says that unsigned invoices are not legally binding and therefore the customer does not have to pay.

Remember it is going to take you twice as long and cost twice as much as you think it will. Although labour is cheap, materials are expensive.

Use Local People:

If you must build, use good local people. Local people, as in any country, know where the best deals and the best workers are, and know how to deal with bureaucrats and work the system. Do not believe a Gringo when they say Ticos do not do good work, are unreliable, lazy or not punctual. In our experience, we have found the opposite to be true, if you have found the right people.

Stay On Site:

We were away for extended periods while construction was supposed to be going on. DO NOT START CONSTRUCTION UNLESS YOU CAN BE PRESENT AT ALL TIMES. Absentee owners are laying themselves wide open to all kinds of problems.

Contract Or Labour Plus Materials:

There are two ways of getting a construction job done in Costa Rica: hire an architect and a contractor and work on a contract basis, or work on a labour plus materials basis. We tried both ways, but unfortunately neither worked for us.

When we wanted to build our guesthouse, we hired an architect and a contractor, made a written contract quoting a price and time of completion. Under a contract arrangement, the architect is responsible for paying the "planilla" which is the amount paid (around 8%) to the "caja" (social security) once a month. If you choose the labour and materials route, the property owner (us) has to pay the "planilla," in addition to labour and materials. Under the contract arrangement, we ended up with a cost

129

over-run of $12,000. Under the labour and materials way, we think our contractor was skimming off a 10% commission at the hardware store and cheating us in other ways.

Three quarters of the way through the project, rumours were swirling around the village that our contractor was entertaining lady friends at our pool during our absence. He was also buying them gold jewellery, and was suspected of taking materials and some of our workers to work on his own house! When we returned from Canada, we were very upset. We were almost finished, the work completed was excellent: the contractor excelled at managing the construction crew and getting the job done. It was now October, almost a year past our scheduled opening, and we desperately needed to be finished by the beginning of December.

Finally we said enough is enough, finish everything by the end of the week and everybody will only get paid when everything is completed. And so it was.

NOTE: A word about "machismo!" I did most of the construction supervision, paid salaries, etc. I had to constantly remind the workers that I was "la jefa" (the boss), but they always insisted on consulting "Don Martin!"

In spite of all the headaches and hassles we went through (many a time we asked ourselves what on earth we were doing here, and maybe we should give it all up!) we have the result we wanted. Our property is beautiful, and we are enjoying every minute of it, GLAD THAT WE DID NOT GIVE UP.

The lesson we learned is this:

- be your own contractor;
- get a costing and stick to it;
- hire sub-contractors step-by-step as needed;
- supervise the project every step of the way;
- do not pay up front;
- pay as work is completed;
- buy your own materials; and
- do not budge from the quoted cost.

Chapter 10
Running a Bed and Breakfast (B & B)

Thinking of running a B & B? Think long and hard before you jump in! The concept of a B & B started in ancient times in Britain, when local families provided food and lodging for a fee when there were no other public inns available for weary travellers. The emphasis is on hospitality in a family setting. Nowadays, the concept varies greatly from the original B & B's.

From the Posada Mimosa guest book:

The view, the accommodations, the breakfast and our hosts – every one perfection. One of the most memorable B&B's we've been to and will definitely remember for years to come.

Ruth & David, Ottawa, Canada

Bill Hemmer and Jeff Crandall, owners of Villa Decary B&B, Lake Arenal

"I like plants and nature, I like people - why not a bed and breakfast? So we pooled all our resources, begged, borrowed and stole and here we are. Surprisingly this building got put up in six months, very fortunate compared to what people say about the speed of Costa Rican builders. We finally had good builders and built from scratch. We had to bring in our own electricity and water. I insisted on city water because having it open to the public, people get leery about ground water. So we dropped $10,000 before we even scratched the surface."

Types of B & B's
Private Homes

This is the true B & B: a family home with a couple of spare bedrooms, and the hosts serve breakfast. Meals other than breakfast may or may not be available. The main emphasis is visiting a local family and, through them, learning about the history and culture of the area.

Family-Run Operations

These include small inns or lodges on a larger scale, owned and operated by a host family who live on site and offer breakfast with the possibility of other meals. The amount of interaction between guest and host varies greatly from family to family, but it is not as close as in a private home.

Commercial Establishments

These include apartment suites, cabins, motels or hotels. The owners do not live on site, so there is no interaction with a host family. They offer breakfast, so technically can call themselves bed and breakfasts, but the friendly, warm environment of a traditional B & B is non-existent.

There are many bed and breakfasts in Costa Rica, ranging from "Mom & Pop" outfits with one or two extra bedrooms, to professionally run businesses which are more like hotels. The true meaning of a bed and breakfast is exactly that: it's not a hotel offering full services, but simply a place to spend the night and enjoy a breakfast the following morning. However, today's travelers expect more, especially in Costa Rica. They expect to be able to send and receive e-mails, and have access to the internet and telephone.

The Advantages and Disadvantages of Running a B & B

Advantages

BE YOUR OWN BOSS. You have total control over the type of guest you want, and when you want to be open or closed or take a holiday. The extra income is a welcome addition and can supplement living expenses, especially in the case of retirees who are usually on fixed incomes.

MEET NEW PEOPLE. It is a great way to meet new people from all over the world and share interests, which can result in personal and business benefits. Life is never boring!

FREE TIME. Once your chores are finished, there is still time left to pursue other interests.

HOUSEHOLD HELP. This is especially a plus in Costa Rica, where help is plentiful and cheap, leaving B & B owners much more free time.

Disadvantages

LESS PRIVACY. Sometimes you want your home to yourself and just enjoy your own company. Some guests are more needy than others and need a lot of attention that may encroach on family time. The best idea is to provide definite times when you are available, and to provide as much written information as possible.

HOUSEKEEPING AND MANAGING STAFF. You must constantly monitor and supervise, ensuring rooms are clean and your staff (if you have one) is doing a proper job. It also means taking inventory on a regular basis – making sure there is enough toilet paper or enough orange juice for breakfast!

BUREAUCRACY. Governments constantly create new rules and regulations, which is especially true in Costa Rica. It is imperative to have a good accountant who can keep you informed of new laws and keep your accounts in order.

SEASONAL UPS AND DOWNS. You need to allow for the slow times, when tourists dry up, along with your income!

Who Is Best Suited To Run a B & B?

While there is no such thing as a "perfect" host, there are certain personal qualities that are more important than others. In our case, we call Martin "the meet and greet tail-wagger," rather like our dachshunds! He genuinely enjoys meeting new people and makes them feel at home. I, on the other hand, am the behind-the-scenes organiser, ensuring that everything runs smoothly. If you are a couple planning to open a B & B, it helps if you have complimentary skills – nobody can be all things to all people.

Some other important qualities:

- BE FRIENDLY, even if you were looking forward to a nice quiet weekend on your own!

- BE TOLERANT, even if it is the umpteenth time you have been asked: "Why did you come to Costa Rica?"

- BE INFORMATIVE about the history and customs of your area, tourist attractions, restaurants, etc. We have an information sheet that eliminates unneces sary repetition.

- BE CLEAN, which means maintaining an interest in housekeeping and a fine eye for small details that make your B & B outstanding. Maintaining our prop erty is probably the most time-consuming aspect of running "Posada Mimosa."

- BE ORGANIZED by thinking ahead and keeping neat and accurate business records.

- BE FLEXIBLE, even though you were not expecting a walk-in!

Chapter 11
Costa Rica Diary and Updates

To give you a better idea of day-to-day living in Costa Rica, here are excerpts from a diary I kept in June 1994, as well as copies of newspaper clippings and newsletters.

Costa Rica Diary

June 22: *We woke up to a beautiful sunny morning and the sounds of birds and workmen hammering. Strangely enough, the hammering was music to our ears - it means progress! The main house is pretty well finished, but the wing has not progressed as fast as we thought! (The original Canadian builders were still on the job at this point.)*

The countryside is green again the flowers and bushes are in bloom, and the grass has grown long. But no problem, the workmen got out their machetes and slashed away and before long it was cut! I think I actually like the rainy season better - tourists should really consider coming here at this time. Jason says scuba diving is at its best now. We met the builders as well as the architect and engineer who brought an artistic rendering of our project. They should finish the wing in three weeks and will start work on the pool and the rancho. We are having a meeting with one of the bureacracies tomorrow to talk about the permit we need to go ahead with the construction of the casitas. Apparently, the powers-that-be are actually enforcing the laws regarding development, making permits much more difficult to obtain. It is their way of stopping over-building, so in a way it is a good thing as long as we get our permits!

From the Posada Mimosa guest book:

*I have never stayed at a place of equal beauty.
The sights, sounds and surroundings are Absolutely beautiful. We loved the "sausage dogs" and the pool. I will never forget our time here.*

*Josh & Jamie,
Los Angeles,
California*

Jason and Martin went shopping to stock up our shelves and spent $70 US for about 10 bags of groceries that included a bottle of vodka and 3 large bottles of wine! In Canada, the vodka and wine would cost $40 US – the vodka here costs $6! The rains came at 4 o'clock and lasted one hour, washing everything clean and the air is so fresh. The rest of the day was sunny and pleasantly warm. The excited staccato tones of the World Cup Soccer commentators drone away on the radio as our workmen hammer away – they seem to be avid fans!

June 23: *We spent all day in San Jose. In order to avoid frustration with the time it takes to accomplish anything here, we decided to set ourselves realistic goals.*

Each day we decide on one or at the most two tasks. The bank was the first place to go because we had not received any statements since Feb. 15. The girl who opened our accounts speaks English, so we went directly to her and one hour later everything was in order. Apparently the bank had sent our statements to a central post office box in San Jose instead of our P.O. Box in Grecia.

While we were in the bank, we saw a couple with badly bruised faces and we could not help staring at them - they looked as if they had been in a car crash! My husband murmured, "plastic surgery I think"! The couple walked by us and said in loud voices "his and her facelifts, we look terrible now, but in four weeks we will be beautiful!" They were Americans who had come to Costa Rica especially for the surgery. Martin said, "I don't think any amount of surgery would make them beautiful, but then beauty is in the eye of the beholder." Elia, who

137

helped us with our banking said, "they look terrible, I will think about them all day and probably all week. I would never do that." I must say I would think twice about doing it too.

We had lunch with our builders and architect in a funky nightclub-restaurant in San Jose, run by a stockbroker from New York and renovated by our builders. I had a chance to talk to Luis, our architect, who said Costa Rica is changing so fast. He said, "It's supposed to be progress - more computers, more machines, more money. But I can understand the old people who don't like the changes. We used to be a relaxed, slow-paced people, but now you can see the strain in people's eyes as they rush around, always in a hurry, always trying to do more and more." After lunch, the rains came as we went to the planning office to tackle the next task. It seems that because we are planning to build four guesthouses on our property for commercial use, we need to have a public road leading into the property. This is a new law that came into effect after our house purchase. It seems laws change every minute. Anyway, we've left it in the hands of our architect to solve. One of our builders says, in practically every case, there is always some kind of glitch and ours is not a big problem. So far we have been pretty lucky I suppose. But, nevertheless, if we can't sort it out, we can't build.

Meanwhile, our workers work really hard from 6 a.m. to 4 p.m. They are excavating to make an office and reception area - it is all done by pick axe. We are paying $180US for five men in their off hours to cut the grass with machetes - about two acres worth. Betty, our maid, does a great job. We have increased her pay to 3,300 colones a week ($21 US). She works five hours a day, five days a week. They get regular 5% raises – the last one

138

was in January and another one was in June. The builders are paying her as well, because she cooks lunch for the workers.

We went for drinks with our next-door neighbours, Ruth and Norma, who are sociologists, and were professors at UCLA. They are trying to grow organic pineapples. After, we went to dinner in La Garita at a restaurant called "Esquina Mariscos" whose specialty is seafood, especially lobster. We tried the lobster that was excellent but much smaller than North American ones.

June 24: We were going to go to the beach this weekend with Jason, but his plans changed so we used today to renew our Bed & Breakfast permit. Martin went to Grecia to see the appropriate person who said we had to change the name on the "patente" from the former owners to our company name. This involved getting the signature of the former owner who is now living in Tilaran on Lake Arenal. We decided to go up and see her and her husband on the weekend.

June 25: It took us about two hours to get to Tilaran. We drove via low-lying Guanacaste that was warm and humid but, after driving 30 minutes into the mountains, the temperature dropped and it was pleasant and cool. The countryside was emerald green and reminded us of the Scottish highlands with its ominous skies and perpetual howling winds. Lake Arenal definitely has a "Loch Ness" quality and the whole area is quite spectacular. We went to dinner at the Hotel Tilawa where we also stayed overnight. The hotel is situated on a hill overlooking the lake and has a fantastic view. It cost $55 US a night without breakfast and we thought it was overpriced especially

139

since this is the low season. The hotel itself is designed to be a replica of the Palace of Knossos in Crete. We have seen the Crete version, and we find it difficult to understand why anyone would recreate it somewhere else in the world! The hotel's atmosphere is not to our taste, and the dining room service is extremely slow.

June 26: We decided to go back via Puntarenas and Jaco beach. Someone had told us that there were beaches north and south of Jaco that were nicer than Jaco. We quickly drove in and out of Puntarenas, a rather dirty town on the edge of the ocean with one small stretch of beach. We saw Playa Herradura, Hermosa and Estrella, and were not terribly impressed. It seems the three beaches at Manuel Antonio are really the nicest in this area. There's no question that the beaches on the Nicoya Peninsula are the best for unspoilt beauty. The beaches on the Caribbean side are far superior to the Jaco area. We are looking for somewhere close to us to avoid the five-hour drive to Nicoya, but so far, we have not found the spot.

The last time we went to Jaco was a year ago, and the main highway was in dreadful shape. Now it is excellent, with fewer potholes than the QEW in Toronto at the end of winter! UNTIL the 10 km stretch before and after Jaco! I cannot understand why they wouldn't fix the most heavily travelled area first. We noticed very few tourists – it's a shame really that people don't come at this time of year – it's so green and lush. We have probably had no more than six hours of rain in a week but have had some spectacular thunderstorms. We have heard that the weather in the Toronto area has been awful – it seems Canadian summers are so unpredictable. And then there are the mosquitoes and black flies. Here in Costa Rica we have no mosquitoes in our area and we have seen no other bugs at all.

June 27: I had an appointment with the President of Rio Tropicales, a large white water rafting company. He never showed up. So we quickly switched to Plan B – fix the car and buy some wicker furniture. We went to El Mundo del Mimbre (mimbre means wicker). There is a huge rattan and wicker factory in San Jose. Excellent quality. We bought two sofas, four chairs, two large coffee tables and two small side tables and a beautiful wicker rocking chair and two foot stools. The total cost was 225,000 colones or $1,451US. They sell sets of two chairs, a sofa and coffee table for prices ranging from 65,000 colones ($420US) and up. We also bought 30 metres of matching fabric for window treatments which cost 39,000 colones ($251US).

June 28: Since we spent all day yesterday in San Jose, we decided to stay in the Grecia area to shop for hardware and groceries. Honestly, it's like starting married life all over again because we are starting from scratch: we need all the simple things like hammers, screw drivers, garden tools. We spent 51,000 colones in the hardware store (around $700 US). Things hard to find here or non-existent and I will bring from Canada: J- cloths, plastic wrap, aluminum foil, bath mats, door mats, shower curtains. They sell tools like axes and rakes without handles. We had to buy the tools for our gardener (we pay him 130 colones an hour – .83 cents!) four hours a day, five days a week.

Of course, we set off on our shopping expedition without a dictionary, as is customary for us, since we are used *to being able to communicate through two other languages and have rarely been in a position of not being able to do so! It really was quite hysterical watching Martin as he "Spanishized" French, threw in some Italian, gesticulated and pantomimed, drew pictures until we had all the Ticos laughing and struggling to comprehend! Who else would go shopping for items without knowing the vocabulary! As an ESL teacher myself, I certainly did not practise what I preach – have a dictionary handy at all times! However we succeeded in getting everything we wanted. We then went off to the "periferico" (supermarket) and spent 13,649 colones to stock up our shelves (roughly $88 US).*

The day ended with a spectacular thunderstorm - it was like a light and sound show! We have a view over the entire valley so we have a marvellous time watching the storms move through. The changing colours of the sky, the dramatic roll of thunder and lightning surpasses any man-made drama! No need for t.v. or movies here - nature puts on a show every night! Twice we have seen double rain-bows!

Then the power went off as I was cooking spaghetti sauce! It was completely black – now I have an idea of what it is like to be blind. Of course, we have no flashlight or candles as yet (both are musts in a country where blackouts are frequent). Jason directed the headlights of the car on the windows for a while. Still no electricity, so there was no alternative but to go to bed. No sooner had we gone to bed, when on came the electricity again – only briefly this time. It was out for about two hours. We subsequently learned that a power transformer went out in the Arenal area plunging the whole country into darkness.

June 29: *It's a holiday today: Dia de San Pedro y San Pablo. There are 8 legal holidays here. Our new furniture arrived – it looks super. Also the concrete mixer came to lay the concrete in our new reception area. We decided to do something about the garden. Since this is the green season or "winter," it is the time to plant so that by "summer" in November, when we come back for an extended period, all our plants should be blooming. We went to Viveros de Laureles in La Garita and came across a very helpful and knowledgeable young man who came to the house and made suggestions about what plants should go where. He measured the area we wanted planted, drew a sketch, took us back to the vivero and showed us the plants we should buy to attract hummingbirds and butterflies. He is going to come out tomorrow with another fellow to do all the planting in one day. We bought 511 plants and 8 bags of earth - it cost $516 US plus $230 for a full day's labour for 3 men! Plants are incredibly cheap. For example: bougainvillea is 150 colones (96 cents) a plant; gardenias are 350 colones ($2.25) each plant; verbena is 100 colones (64 cents) a plant. The most expensive plant was 1,000 colones ($6.45).*

June 30: *Another beautiful morning. No rain yesterday. Today we are going shopping for bathroom tiles and whatever else we need to complete renovations. Our builder took us to three tile places that had pretty good selections. He came to Costa Rica from northern B.C. and lives in the Cariari development. He said since he came here the value of a lot in his area has increased 5 times! He said Costa Rica is definitely in a boom period that will probably last another three years and then he thinks it will slow down. As far as buying real estate goes, he says* *more people are buying land for speculation rather than buying existing housing. He said if he had bought enough land four years ago, he would be a multi-millionaire today!*

Every time we come down we see more and more development. I'm not sure if that's necessarily a good thing. Prices have gone up and the cost of groceries has increased. For example, a pre-cooked chicken costs 800 colones ($5.16). We pay our gardener the equivalent of 4 chickens a week! Is that fair? He works very hard and deserves more but he set the salary. One wonders what the eventual effect will be on Costa Ricans whose salaries don't keep pace with the rise in the cost of living. There's a widening gap between "have's" and "have-nots" and we hope it won't lead to a "Mexican syndrome." One wonders if the pace of progress will change the gentle nature of the people.

July 1: Canada Day! There are two Canadian clubs here and both held celebrations today. The original club called The Canadian Club was started years ago by Harry Cooper but recently, some members split and formed another club called The Canadian Club of Costa Rica Association, headed by Phil McColl. According to a spokesman at the Canadian-Costa Rican Chamber of Commerce, the mandate of the Canadian Club is social and service and not commercial. However, the Canadian Club of Costa Rica Association offers medical insurance to its members which is regarded as a commercial activity. Both clubs are officially recognized by the Canadian embassy.

We had lunch with a German friend of Jason's who is going back to Germany very reluctantly after four months here. She says she can't live in Germany any more after taking this year off to travel. People there cannot possibly understand why she wants to live in Costa Rica. She says she feels so free and light since she left her rather materialistic culture. She says all anybody cares about is how much money they make and what car they drive. She plans to sell everything and return in the fall. We meet so many people who feel the same way. They are like refugees from the culture of greed.

We did some banking that we now do with easy familiarity. It's like everything in Costa Rica, if you follow the system and rhythm of life here, it really is very logical and makes a lot of sense. For example, people here rise with the sun, work hard all morning, stop at noon when it's hot and everything shuts down for siesta time until two o'clock, then go back to work until five o'clock. It gets dark about six o'clock, so it's early to bed.

After the bank, we picked up our two wicker end tables and headed back to Jason's dive shop. They were all there watching soccer in this soccer-mad country. Apparently, Costa Rica had a team at the world championships four years ago and they seem to be rooting for Brazil or Argentina - Latin American solidarity, I guess. We had to wait while our car was once again being fixed. Car repairs are expensive here. A few more people came into the shop – a chiropractor from Texas who was going diving with Ecotreks on the weekend. It was his first visit here and he is planning to set up a chiropractic association to set standards and regulate the profession. Laws for it are non-existent at the moment. I asked him why he planned to live in Costa Rica. He said: "to escape racism and crime in Dallas." He said crime has a new twist now – it is called car-jacking or car-napping. Criminals follow you home to your driveway, hold you up with a gun, take your car and whatever contents you may have in the car as well as your money. (Note: In 1996 this was also happening in certain areas of San Jose.) He asked us why we had decided on Costa Rica. We said "taxes, health care and climate" in that order!

We joked about how everyone is waiting for something in Costa Rica – an appointment, waiting in line at the bank, residency papers etc. But is it better anywhere else anymore? Another truism is that nothing is for sale in Costa Rica but everything can be bought at a price. You ask Mr. Rodriguez: "I would like to buy your property for $300,000." He responds: "It's not for sale, I'm leaving it to my son." A few minutes later he says he might sell if the price is right!

Our garden was planted today – it's only a start but it already looks much better. We bought plants which will attract butterflies and hummingbirds – verbena, once de Abril which has blue flowers and orange berries, bougainvillea, plantanillas, urucas, gardenias, pileas, galanchoes – I don't know the names in English. Now is the time to plant so that by November everything will be flourishing, if the leaf-cutting ants don't demolish them!

July 2: Today we went on the warpath against the ants! They have already mobilized and are starting to eat our new plants. They may be charming in the rain forest but they are not in our garden! They can strip bushes overnight. So our mission was to find something to exterminate them. After an hour of looking we finally found the antidote. When we got back to the house, our workers were all waiting to go home but when they saw us with our spraying machine etc., they offered to do the job for us. In no time they tracked down all the offending anthills and within hours there was no sign of any ants. Mission *accomplished! But you have to continually watch out for them because they will regroup again. We are conscientious environmentalists but, if we let the ants take over, we will have no flowers for the birds and butterflies - so it's a bit of a dilemma.*

July 3: *Today we are taking it easy finishing up the bits and pieces before we leave for Canada again in two days. It's been rather heavy and humid the last couple of days and not much sunshine. One important thing I've discovered is that if you are a light sleeper like I am, do not forget to bring some wax earplugs. It is never quiet here – birds, howler monkeys in the jungle, roosters at all hours of the day and night, the sounds of nature never stop – add a few more man-made noises. After a few days we get used to it and settle in fine. But if you find yourselves in San Jose, you could be driven to distraction with the noise of traffic, honking horns etc. Of course, if you live in a big city, you may be used to it.*

We decided to go to Sarchi and price some leather rocking chairs (approximately $58 US). We really like the drive – around every corner there's a beautiful view. I had always wanted to see the famous garden at Zarcero with all the sculpted hedges. The hills are covered with coffee plantations and, as you climb higher, it changes to dairy farms with Holstein and Jersey cattle instead of the Brahmins that are found on the hot, humid coastal areas. The highest point was 1800 metres (5,000 feet), very cool and cloudy. It was like being in another country, a lot like Switzerland. On our way back, we went a different way via San Ramon and ran into very thick clouds. The nice part about living in this area is the many interesting places to see without having to drive too far.

July 4: US Independence Day. The American Embassy invited 5,000 people (you have to hold a US passport) for a picnic. For the last three days, the weather has been muggy and cloudy, not as nice as when we first arrived. Today, we are getting ready to leave tomorrow for Canada. I'm rather reluctant to leave my garden to the mercy of the leaf-cutting ants which have reappeared! Our gardener is going to buy some granular stuff that is supposed to get rid of them and will definitely keep an eye on them. We really have accomplished a lot on this trip - everything we set out to do.

We read recently that Carlos Roesch has been appointed the new Minister of Tourism and is very interested in promoting ecotourism and sustainable development and plans a much more aggressive marketing strategy to achieve his goals. The two faces of Costa Rica - the tourist one and the "real" Costa Rica - have always left me somewhat unsettled. While touting the pristine beauty of the country and preservation of the trees, the "real" Costa Rica is one of smoke-belching trucks and buses which should not be allowed on the road, the polluted air of San Jose which makes one's eyes sting, the noise of traffic and honking horns and planes shattering the silence with take-offs and landings during the night, the polluted rivers and oceans and garbage-strewn countryside.

To preserve its reputation, the first thing the Minister of Tourism should do is meet with the Ministry of Transport and Public Works and pass stringent laws to correct all of the afore-mentioned before making any marketing attempts. To quote Mr. Roesch: "Investors are welcome as long as they play by the rules of the game", he told Costa Rica Today, "we don't want to make compromises. If a company is planning to make an investment in a project that doesn't fit our concept of sustainable develop-

ment, we're sorry, but they will have to go to another country". I agree, Mr. Roesch, but you also have a big job ahead of you cleaning up Costa Rica's own backyard. (N.B. Since these words were written in 1994, the Figueres government has made tremendous strides in cracking down on polluters with new laws and heavy fines.)

In the Costa Rican Press
(Costa Rica Today - June 30, 1994)

According to 1993 statistics from CINDE more than half of the tourists from Europe, Canada and the United States visit during the rainy season from May until November. Europeans stay the longest time with approximately 60 percent of them staying more than 22 nights each year, while only 23 percent of Canadians and 14 percent of Americans stay about the same time. The average length of stay for Canadians is about two weeks and for Americans a little more than one week. Most come for pleasure and vacation while about 20 percent come for business. Tourists spend on average $15-$85 a day on food, sightseeing and souvenirs.

End to Monopoly of State Banks

After many years of debate and study, the end of the monopoly held by state banks is near. Though reforms in recent years have granted increased liberalization in the banking sector, commercial banks were prohibited access to the checking account business. Now, a congressional subcommittee has endorsed the plan of permitting private commercial banks to compete in this market. The new law will be put to a vote in the legislature within a year.

149

Travel Statistics

Tourist arrivals in Costa Rica constitute a wide spectrum of nationalities. A breakdown shows that in the first half of 1998:

Origin	Tourists	%
U.S.	231,551	45%
Europe	103,643	20%
Central America	51,580	10%
South America	47,000	9%
Canada	42,685	8%
Other	33,050	6%

Language Classes for Schools

A new plan to teach French and English to elementary school children was announced this past week. The program will begin with 9,000 students in grades one through three and 40 teachers and is scheduled to begin July 18. The program will begin in 27 education centres selected because they are in poor areas near tourism destinations or factories that concentrate on exporting. The goal by 1998 is to teach 100,000 students English and 23,000 French, plus train 500 teachers.

Update: December 1994
Our Property

Since our last newsletter in August, we have been back and forth to Costa Rica to monitor progress on our ongoing renovations. After months of frustration, we had to fire our contractor due to non-performance. Of course, we trusted too much which is easy to do with your own countrymen when you are in a strange country.

So what to do? We had to make the best of a bad situation. The first step was to find new people to finish the project; we had already wasted too much time. Our lawyer recommended one of his architect friends and one of our Costa Rican neighbours rounded up a crew of workers from our area. The good news is that Grecia and surroundings has a reputation for having the best workers in Costa Rica. Edgar Rojas, the architect, was very professional and businesslike and guaranteed that the wing of the house would be completed by December 10 and that we would pay by the week as the work was being completed.

So far, we are very impressed with our totally "Tico" crew led by an ex-school principal, who is a veritable whirling dervish as he keeps the workers going from 6 a.m. to 5 p.m. including Saturdays! At the same time, our pool is almost finished and so is the "rancho." We are going down with all our furniture on December 9 to start our new adventure. Our first guests for our bed and breakfast will arrive at the end of December and we have some more people coming in January. We could have fully booked November and December if we had been ready.

In spite of the obstacles that blocked our progress, we are still happy with our decision and are sure our property will be wonderful when the work is finished. We are putting the past behind us and looking forward to enjoying every minute in Costa Rica.

Embassy Update

I spoke to an official at the Costa Rican Embassy in Ottawa, to get some statistics about Canadians in Costa Rica. He said they expected 62,000 Canadian tourists to visit the country during 1994. In 1995, they were predicting 80,000. Most Canadians prefer to visit rain forests, national parks, volcanoes and river rafting rather than the beaches. He said many bird-watchers and tropical and medicinal plant researchers are interested in Costa Rica.

Generally, people first visit as tourists then they think of retiring and/or investing. "It surprises me that so many Canadians, because they have heard what a beautiful country it is, decide to go and live there without first visiting or having any knowledge of the country," he said. "I strongly advise people to first go and see." Canadians generally invest in tourism - hotels, restaurants and travel agencies - rather than agricultural or industrial enterprises. Americans top the list as the largest investors, followed by Germans who have been a presence for many years, and Canadians in third place. Mr. Gonzalez predicts that in 3-5 years the number of Canadian investors will surpass the Germans. When I asked him about the sharp increase in entrance fees to parks and rain forests, he said that Costa Rican fees were far too low compared to other countries and, in order to help preserve the ecosystems, the numbers of visitors have to be curtailed and fees increased to improve the administration of the parks and forests.

Beaches Update

On our last trip in October, although we only had 10 days, we really wanted to find a beach other than Jaco that we could get to in an hour or so from our house. We finally found it – Playa Esterillos – it is just after Playa Hermosa and before Parrita. It is exactly what we were looking for: miles of light sand stretches in both directions with simple weather-beaten houses right on the beach, nary a condo or high-rise in sight – utterly unspoiled. If you are looking for peace and quiet, it is the perfect spot. It is not well marked on the road, and we went right by the tiny sign (Esterillos Oeste), ending up in Parrita before realizing we had gone too far.

On this trip, we stayed overnight at Punta Leona Hotel & Club that is near Tarcoles, north of Jaco, close to the Carara Biological Reserve. The approach to the club is unspoilt jungle, very well maintained, and there are three beaches to choose from. The setting is beautiful, but we were not too impressed with the architecture and configuration of this large development of rooms, apartments and condos. If you are looking for long stretches of white sand beaches, you will find them in Guanacaste province on the Pacific coast.

Among the many areas of Guanacaste offering first class accommodations in addition to beautiful beaches are:
Playa Grande, Playa Conchal, Playas del Coco, Playa Flamingo, Garza, Playa Hermosa, Samara and Nosara.
All these can be reached by car from San Jose and will take between 3.5 and 4.5 hours. They can also be reached by plane.
Charter flights from Toronto and Montreal fly directly to Liberia airport that is a 30 minutes bus ride from Playa Flamingo.

153

Chapter 12
"Summer" Ends, "Green" Seasons Begins – Updates After The Move

Letters to Our Friends and Family

The birth of our tenth grandchild, Camille, at the end of March, has brought us back to Canada to do our grand parenting tours of Montreal, Calgary and Toronto.

In a series of faxes to Canada, I related our progress after our move in December 1994. These letters provide good insight into our thoughts while adjusting to a new country.

January 3, 1995

Hello Everybody!

Now that the dust has settled (figuratively speaking – our construction crews continue to be with us), things are much calmer and more organized. We had a very hectic three weeks and, at one point, we even considered not unloading the furniture and putting it on the next boat back! Megan, Paul and children landed in the middle of all the unpacking, but in spite of it all, they seemed to have really enjoyed it here. Megan even considered missing the plane, and Paul suggested he become our manager with a little house on the property and get out of the rat race!

Little Tessa (the workers all called her "Tessita") was the star attraction (blue eyes and blonde hair will do it every time here!). Costa Ricans really adore children.

From the Posada Mimosa guest book:

What a beautiful sight to behold as we drove up to your casa! The beautiful view from every vantage point was muy Hermosa!! Loved the swim, the fall of evening shade, our quarto,

Your Claudio and Betty. Hate to depart! Muchas gracias!

Audrey & Paul, Mississauga, Ontario, Canada

Unfortunately, the Jourdain family arrived with coughs and colds and I ended up with a form of the flu. I slept 24 hours straight and had it beaten in three days. I think my body was rebelling at everything I had put it through over the last few months and it finally said "enough already!"

Our first guests were the Strobele family from Oakville. I met Marianne at the University Women's Club when I first arrived in Oakville. She and her husband Kurt are originally from Namibia in Africa (formerly German Southwest Africa). They couldn't get over the similarity between the landscape in our area and South Africa. They came with their teenaged daughters Evita and Claudia. We could not have asked for better guests – they were interesting, interested in everything, and loved our place. The only tiresome thing was they arrived in the middle of my flu bout, but Martin took over, did a super job, and has become renowned for his German pancakes!

We were invited to a New Year's Eve party at the house of the fellow who made our beds and other furniture. Luis Angel is quite a character – he is an "artiste" – he sings, paints and lives in a castle! Apparently, he visited Spain once and saw the castle of one of the kings and decided he had to have a castle himself. So there it sits on a hill on the way to Sarchi - gleaming white and rather incongruous in these surroundings! He's now designing a maze of plants a la Hampton Court in his back garden! The Strobeles went along and found it very interesting and a New Year's Eve they won't forget!

We had ten people for Christmas dinner: Jason and friends, our two American neighbours, retired professors in their mid-fifties from UCLA who are now into organic pineapple farming. It was probably one of our best Christmases in spite of the fact that we had no tree, no

Christmas pudding or decorations, the place was full of boxes, but somehow the chemistry of all the people worked.

Now about the property. The garden has survived the leaf-cutting ants and is looking great. This being the dry season (it won't rain for the next four months!) we really have to do a lot of watering. The most important things to have here are water, a gardener and a maid. Our first oranges will be ready to be picked soon, ditto the bananas. Megan said the pool is the best one she has ever swum in. It really is the greatest thing to have here because it gets pretty hot in the middle of the day. Now that the holidays are over we are starting to get into a routine of sorts. We get up at 7 a.m., go for a walk and a swim, have breakfast and deal with whatever comes up. We swim again around 3 p.m., always stop for tea at 4 p.m. and the hour between 5 and 6 p.m. is sacred, nothing interferes with as we watch some incredible sunsets. All the rooms look great with the drapes and duvets we brought down, though our office still has to be finished. We have been very disappointed with our pool company which is building the rancho – it still is not finished and so many mistakes have been made, they have had to redo things two or three times.

Jason and company are extremely busy, both at their beach location and at their shop in Escazu. In the next few days he will take 42 people mountain biking through Santa Rosa National Park, most of them are in their 60's and 70's - Jason says that's the age group of most of his mountain bikers! On one of his trips he rides down the face of a volcano after driving the people up but he says some of them even ride all the way up to the volcano! Jason's shop is amazing, they've made it look like a jungle – he and his partners did all the construction and design.

January 6, 1995

Dear Hilary -

Construction is moving along – finally had all the construction mess vacuumed out of the pool that now looks perfect. They have had to remove the tiles in the rancho three times now and will have to redo the bar-b-q and smokehouse. We tried it the other day and it promptly cracked in four places – so they spent the afternoon destroying it! It has really been a damned nuisance –it all was supposed to be finished before Christmas! However, we don't get as frustrated as we did when we first arrived –we are adjusting to Manana-land!

January 10, 1995

Dear Megan and Paul -

Here, we are getting more and more relaxed - so much better than when you were here. We finally told the pool company to take a walk (we later changed our minds) - nothing improved - all the tiles taken up again, etc., etc. So now Edgar, our architect, is drawing up a costing that we will claim back from them. Here we go again! The bodega (storage house) is finished this Friday, which means we can put away a lot of stuff and it will force us to deal with the boxes. We've got a lot of mirrors and pictures up but we still have masses of photographs to go.

This week we have a couple of Franco-Ontarians who have just moved to Vancouver staying with us. They are a very nice and interesting couple who are thinking of retiring here. He is a retired school principal from near Timmins and he said last year it was –34C for two months! He said that did it for him so he moved to Vancouver to be with his girlfriend. They got engaged down

157

here and both have read The Celestine Prophecy and he is also into homeopathic medicine.

Now that we are both unstressed and feeling fit, we really look forward to having guests. I have got breads (banana, chocolate, lemon, pineapple and carrot) that are delicious. So today I served (yes, I'm doing breakfast!) a big bowl of pineapple, papayas, bananas, grapes and tangerines with granola, Betty's "gallo pinto" (rice, beans and eggs) - they really enjoyed it. Tomorrow, it's pancakes. Next week we are expecting an elderly threesome, then some friends from Prague and Montreal. So far all the people have come from the newsletter. Nobody seems to mind that construction is still going on. So life is really pleasant especially when we get weather reports from Canada saying how cold it is! I was quite right about getting positive reinforcement on a regular basis - everybody who has come here just thinks it's fantastic!

January 10, 1995

Dear Hilary & Pierre

Regarding your in-laws. For them to get the most out of their two weeks here, we recommend that they spend one week with us exploring the area around here and then go travelling down the Pacific coast.They could go to Manuel Antonio, the Osa Peninsula and work their way up to the Gulf of Nicoya and the Flamingo beach area. Bed and breakfast accommodation is plentiful and cheaper than the hotels but, of course, they might want to stay in a resort for a night or two. But they will really see a fair amount of Costa Rica that way. It is much hotter on the coast but there are always ocean breezes so that you don't feel it all that much. We could plan their trip if we knew what their interests are - national parks? rainforests, cloud forests?

158

sports? nature & wildlife? turtles? There is so much to do here and you will never see it all in one visit. So it is important to have a fair idea of what they want to do. For instance, there is a trip we want to do on an aerial tramway through a rain forest (Braulio Carillo), expensive and I have heard mixed reports about it. The volcanoes are a must, especially Arenal which would require an overnight because it is best to see at night. Poas volcano is about an hour and a half from us and would be a half-day trip. Also there are hikes near us into forests with waterfalls, etc. So, it's a matter of booking a charter flight (Megan said Canadian Holidays was terrific but I don't know if they fly out of Montreal), preferably out of the high season (March) because the rates are slightly lower. There is also an 18-hole golf course about 20 minutes from us.

January 10, 1995

Dear Matthew

Each morning Grammy takes a swim at 7 a.m. and at that time we have seen toucans in the trees on our property not too far from the pool. They make a strange sort of clucking sound, not really very musical, but it tells you they are about somewhere. So you follow the sound, I now take binoculars with me and sure enough there they are eating the fruit off the trees. They especially like mangoes, although they are not in season now but they also like other fruits too. They are a brilliant yellow and black but are rather shy so you have to be very quiet if you want to see them. The other day Opi saw two huge iguanas on the path down towards the river. Costa Ricans like to eat them because they taste a lot like chicken! This is the dry season or summer and it will not rain at all for the next four

159

months so that's the time when you really see the wildlife because they are in search of water and food. It's a full time job chasing dust because it's so dry and our maid has to clean the house every day - it's a never-ending battle! When Megan was here, we experienced our first earthquake tremors - there was an earthquake south of San Jose and we felt the tremors here. Everything started rattling, it was really weird!

Dear Heidi -

Have you read The Celestine Prophecy? You must read it, it's most interesting - it gives nine insights into the next millenium and describes what is occurring now in the final days of this millenium - fascinating. Maurice and Suzanne, our guests at the moment, have read the book and go off to seminars, stress management workshops using all kinds of different therapies such as dance therapy. They are in touch with the Eastern religions and know a lot of people who lead spiritual renewal workshops, so we are hoping to put together a group to come down here. I find this whole field of natural medicine, spiritual renewal etc. quite fascinating and it is certainly the "in" thing at the moment as people realize the purely materialistic no longer satisfies them. Maurice and Suzanne are looking into buying a farm in Dominical near the ocean.

January 20, 1995

Hallo Everybody!

We've made a lot of progress this week with the construction. The pool people finally got their act together and rebuilt the BBQ and have put down new tiles. The "bodega" is just about finished and next week they start on our

160

reception area and office. We have such nice people staying here this week - three people in their '70's. They go off
every day with the car and driver I organized (it costs $50
per day plus expenses) and they are very pleased with
everything. They want to see as much as possible in a
week because, as they say, who knows how much longer
we'll be around!

Children here are on holiday now - they are off school
for three months! Some of the construction workers bring
their children to the site (can you imagine the occupation-
al health people in Canada hearing that!) I'm suffering
from news withdrawal - I haven't read a newspaper since
I've been here or seen any news on t.v. Hilary faxes us
pretty well every day re business and told us about the
Canadian dollar and that the IMF might take over
Canadian finances like they did in New Zealand in 1984.
We are reading a book called "Take Your Money and Run!"
- it's all about how to legally avoid paying taxes!

My newsletter brings people here - two fellows
dropped in the other day - one is living here and the other
is a farmer from Saskatchewan who had a terrible sun-
burn but really loved C.R. We are going to solve the
"news" problem today or tomorrow - somebody is coming
to install some sort of box which will cost $150 and you
get all the channels you want including CNN and then you
don't pay any more after that - no monthly cable bills.
Every day we pick oranges off the trees, we also have
banana trees, lemons and tangerines. Our Spanish is coming along very well, of course we make a lot of mistakes,
but we have no choice because people here don't speak
English. I almost forgot, the biggest news of all - we have
a little dachshund (our "guard" dog!). All the guests and
workers love him!

February 1, 1995

Dear Mimi and Gilles (Hilary's in-laws)

We went to Flamingo Beach last week and looked around at various hotels etc. We found that everybody was complaining because the number of tourists has dropped off so the hotels are not full. Usually in March it picks up again. The hotel we like the best is Hotel Sugar Beach - it has its own light sandy beach, safe swimming, has the best rooms I've seen and the food is excellent. It is very quiet and you would have to drive about 10 minutes if you wanted to try other restaurants. The roads leading to all the hotels are abominable, I don't understand why they don't fix them. The other hotel nearer (by 5 minutes) to restaurants is the Hotel Potrero (Canadian-owned), the rooms are not as nice but are o.k. The beach is black sand which you may or may not like but it is safe to swim. The Potrero has a pool, the Sugar Beach does not but it is surrounded by nature and animal life. If you book through Jason, he gets a discount. The rate he gets is $70 for a double room with one double bed at the Sugar Beach and $96.50 for a double room at the Potrero. There are cabinas too which cost half but believe me, when you have driven four hours and it's hot and you have bounced along the washboard roads once you get off the main highway, you will appreciate comfort and peace and quiet! The main highway is pretty good except for some potholes but that's Costa Rica!

February 1, 1995

Hi Peggy!

I just received your letter dated January 18, so it took about 12 days to get here. Life here continues to be a whirl of construction - they are now working on our office.

The original office the Canadian company had built had to be all torn down - needless to say we were very discouraged and the dust and mess was awful. I think the Costa Rican crew we have now must think they are in the "destruction" business instead of construction! The good thing is that they are fantastic workers and have got more done in three months than the Canadians did in six! Tomorrow we are going to work on landscaping. We are putting in lots of palm trees and tropical plants around the pool. Everything is blooming like crazy, I can't understand why because no rain has fallen and none will until April. We have to put down grass and cover up all the exposed earth that creates all the dust. Martin has been suffering with the most irritating cough for the last four weeks and finally went to the doctor who said he thinks he's probably allergic to all the dust. He's rather frustrated today because we have not been able to make any international phone calls or send and receive faxes.

When we were at Flamingo Beach last the hotels were not full and they are all wondering why. I think I can tell them why. Apparently, as is usually the case when tourism develops too fast, crime is on the rise especially on the Caribbean coast where an American woman was murdered in November and some others have been raped. So the US and Canadian embassies have issued warnings which really is a bit ironic considering that in the whole of last year in Costa Rica, there were only 25 murders whereas we all know the crime statistics in the US. However, it's a good idea to tell people to be cautious as you would in any country. The problem here is that Costa Rica has such a clean image that people get careless. We rarely drive long distances at night and wouldn't dream of camping on a beach and that's when these incidents happened.

The increased park fees are the biggest problem - there are two prices, one for locals and one for tourists. The local pay $1.00 to go to a national park for a day and tourists are charged $15 ($25 Can.) which is outrageous. There are a lot of protests in the press and from the travel industry - after all you don't kill the goose that laid the golden egg and tourism is the number one industry and everyone's bread and butter. So something must happen soon. Add the abominable roads leading to the resort hotels and you have a problem. (N.B. In 1996, tourism officials realized the folly of their ways and changed the prices back to what they were).

This time of year they cut the sugar cane and some farmers burn it even though it's against the law. So the sweet smell of burning cane hangs over everything and drops cinders into our pool! There's an environmental group in Grecia that is trying to stop it. The cane is not cut all at the same time, so the fields are constantly changing patterns because the cane starts growing again almost as soon as it is cut. So you have fields in varying stages of new growth and the view we have changes constantly because of the variety of hues of green.

March 7, 1995

Hi Megan!

I called a halt to construction for Monday and Tuesday this week and it is just heaven having the peace and quiet. We really have had enough and didn't want the banging and hammering for Helga, Mimi and Gilles. They call our place "le Paradis"! The office is coming along beautifully; they have done a great job. It's still a continuing battle with the ants as they attack new plants so Lacqui (our gardener) is on the warpath daily. This being the driest point of the dry season, Lacqui spends half of his time watering. Around the pool, we have used mostly small palms, grasses, white stones, exora (small orange plant), verbena and bougainvillaea. The ants come out at night only so it is not easy to find their nests. We are probably going to take a hot air balloon ride on March 16 along with Mimi and Gilles.

"Two Wonderful Weeks in Costa Rica"

A letter from Micheline and Gilles Leonard,
Mount Royal, Quebec.

As the aircraft descended into its final approach to Juan Santamaria airport, our first close-up view of Costa Rica was very impressive. The valley was surrounded by mountains rising beyond small clouds that seemed to cling to the ridges, fields of sugar cane and coffee along the mountain sides, and dirt roads winding all the way up to the ridges. It would have been regrettable to have this first impression spoiled by an immediate stay in the capital city of San Jose. It is much more preferable to stay at an inn or a bed and breakfast where one can establish headquarters to visit the area. We went immediately to Posada Mimosa, a bed and breakfast in the village of Rincon de Salas, near Grecia where, at an altitude of 750 meters, the 270-degree view over the valley with the mountains as a backdrop, is simply breathtaking and the accommodations homey and luxurious. We immediately fell in love with Costa Rica.

From this location, there are many points of interest that can be visited, including San Jose. Small municipalities like Grecia, Sarchi and Naranjo are not only pleasant to visit, but the roads leading to these places offer a true *close-up look at the magnificent countryside and the way people live. We visited such places as Poas Volcano, Zoo Ave (Bird Zoo), Zarcero where we met Evangelisto Blanco who sculptures all the hedges into animal shapes, the forest and waterfall called Los Choros, just beyond a small village called Bambi, and the Los Angeles Cloud Forest which is every bit as beautiful as Monteverde minus the crowds and almost impassable roads leading to Monteverde.*

We rented a 4 x 4 air-conditioned jeep that we paid for in Canada and then travelled to the active Arenal Volcano. We greatly enjoyed the itinerary followed across the mountains between the Central and Tilaran ranges via Naranjo, Zarcero, Quesada and Fortuna. We stayed at the foot of the volcano at Arenal Observatory Lodge and lived a unique experience. We kept hearing the rumbling of the volcano, we saw flames leaping hundreds of feet above the volcano at 1.30 a.m., we were awakened by howler monkeys at 5.30 a.m. and saw a beautiful sunrise on the volcano and Lake Arenal. We walked to a 1992 lava flow and found the lava too hot to handle only 6 inches below the surface. All of this, including bird watching in a tropical forest was an amazing experience. Some of the tourists staying at the lodge went to another side of the volcano at night where they could see the red lava flowing from the top.

The next day, after a dip in the thermal baths in Tabacon with the volcano in the background, we travelled to Monteverde following the paved road around Lake Arenal (full of surprises!) to the town of Tilaran. From there, we began a 35km stretch over a "gravel" road that took us 2-1/2 hours to negotiate via Quesera and Santa Elena. We did not believe such roads could exist! Nothing but potholes and stones (we welcomed the occasional gravel sections) of all sizes and shapes, many with sharp edges and points. We were particularly concerned about potential flat tires, but we managed. The views, however, were magnificent.

Our stay at Monteverde was very enjoyable including our guided excursion into the cloud forest, observations of many birds and tropical vegetation. We did not get to see a Quetzal which was most unusual. In Monteverde, there was a foul-up with our advance reservation at Hotel Fonda Vela but we were very comfortable at the Hotel de Montana. We left Monteverde the next day for the Pacific coast travelling the other leg of the "gravel" road via Guaria and Sarmiento. A funny surprise just outside of Santa Elena: a toll-booth and a fee of 100 colones for the privilege of using that road! Again, stones, rocks, potholes, but in addition, a winding road up the mountains and along the ridges with no guard rails and precipices (more than 1,000 feet drops) less than 10 feet (it looked like 2 to 3 feet only) from the edge of the narrow, curving road. But the views were absolutely marvellous! This time, it only took us 1-1/2 hours to negotiate less than 30 km of this road, always on the 4-wheel drive. What an experience! The kind of driving experience you come out of and feel proud to have accomplished and grateful that the car also made it without mishap. We enjoyed Monteverde very much and we do not regret the unique experience and magnificent views. However, if one prefers easier access roads, we are certain that other similar cloud forests can be reached along more conventional roads.

We then spent four days at a location that has to be very close to paradise. This was at Hotel Sugar Beach on Playa Pan de Azucar on the shores of the Pacific. Truly an *intimate getaway directly on a beautiful white sandy beach with comfortable rooms and gourmet dining overlooking the ocean. Again, morning awakening by howler monkeys that could be observed from the beach, many varieties of birds and what spectacular sunsets! We also visited Tamarindo and Flamingo.*

We returned to Posada Mimosa travelling via Santa Cruz, Mansion, then up to Puerto Moreno where we took the ferry across the northern tip of the Gulf of Nicoya, and then south along the Inter-American highway. Once more, the scenery was spectacular and the driving an experience, as always in Costa Rica.

With a wonderful rest at Posada Mimosa for the end of our holidays, we capped off this wonderful trip with a unique and marvellous experience - a hot air balloon ride over the valley at sunrise from Naranjo to beyond Grecia. Breakfast and a visit of Orcafe coffee plantation followed this. And to top off this splendid day, at suppertime we received a fax announcing the birth of our grandson (grandchild #5 for us) which we celebrated in joy with our wonderful hosts with champagne, compliments of the house!

Chapter 13
Epilogue

Our daughter Megan wrote the following letter to her nieces and nephew as they were about to embark on their new life in New Zealand, moving from Calgary Alberta. Megan is a race relations specialist and holds a Master's degree in multicultural studies. She is also an ESL/EFL teacher and teaches English teachers who are going abroad how to feel comfortable living in a new country and what kinds of feelings and changes to expect. She has lived in Japan where she set up a private English school and has also lived in France and Germany. Toronto is her home where she lives with her husband and three children. Although this letter has been simplified especially for children, its sentiments also apply to adults. It was recently published in the Tico Times.

"Dear Matthew, Alex, Caitlin and Jessica,

First, let me say that you are very lucky to have the experience of living in a new country. As you grow up, you will be able to look back on how you managed the changes in your life, and it will make you ready for anything that you want to do!! It will make you stronger people!

There are many stages you will go through as you adjust to being in a new culture, a new country, a new environment. The thing to remember is that all your feelings are very important and are part of the process of starting something new.

Because you have moved to a new place as a family, it is really important that you respect that some of your family might not be feeling the same way as you. Be kind and patient with each other because it is your family that will help you the most!

When you arrive in your new home it will feel like being on vacation. You will be excited about all the things that are new and you will want to explore. You will compare New Zealand with Canada in a positive way. You will say something like "Hey! The cars are different. That's neat!" It is like getting a new pair of shoes that look really cool and fashionable. You might feel good like this for 5 hours or 5 months, it is different for everybody.

As time goes by, everything new that excited you really starts to bug you. You get tired of trying to figure everything out all the time. Your brain gets fed up with taking in all the differences. You might start having problems because you don't know how things are done in New Zealand and you have to learn. You might try to solve problems the way you used to in Canada but it doesn't work in New Zealand. This will make you frustrated. You will want to have things the way they were and you will start feeling homesick for Canada and all the things that were comfortable to you. You might feel like there is no hope and you will never like your new country. The new shoes that looked so cool before are giving your feet blisters and you are thinking of throwing them out!

It is really important to understand why you will feel so sad and crabby at this point. I'll explain why ....

We spend our whole life, even if we are only 8 years old, building who we are. We do this in a lot of ways: by becoming part of a neighbourhood, being part of a swim team, being a member of a club at school, making really good friendships, being part of a group of kids at school, having favourite teachers and neighbours, having favourite parks and places to play, decorating a room just the way you like it, having a favourite TV program, having a special boyfriend or girlfriend, having and taking care of pets, *being part of a family. All these people and places form a web and you are the big fat spider and they support you in that web!*

When you arrive in a new country, the people and places that made you feel like you belonged and made up your cosy web are not there. Everything has changed and you have to build up your web again to make you feel at home.

During this crabby time, you will be really mad at someone or even at the whole country of New Zealand, sheep included! We all need a lightning rod when we are really feeling stressed and unhappy. Because you are a family going through this together, you will all be each other's lightning rod at one point. The important thing to do during this time is to remember to talk about your feelings, apologise when necessary and forgive each other. And remember that this part won't last forever, and soon when you have built your web, you will feel really good.

Gradually the bad times will pass and you will start to feel comfortable in your surroundings. They won't seem so new any more. You know how things work and your brain will start processing things automatically. The differences around you won't jump out at you any more.

That cool pair of shoes is not giving you blisters any more and you are starting to enjoy them! Your web is starting to look good and after experimenting a bit you have found a good spot in it to catch the best tasting flies.

When you walk down the street you see familiar faces. At school, kids and teachers know who you are and what you can do. Your new room is starting to look the way you want it. Maybe you have made a new best friend or you have discovered a really neat bike path. You have figured out the TV schedule and you have some favourite shows.

You are starting to laugh at the things that made you uncomfortable before. You do not need your lightning rod as much.

You will actually start to like all those annoying differences that bugged you before. You are on your way to feeling really good and confident about your new life and your place in it.

I hope all this makes sense to you. Maybe it won't right now but it will when you are going through it. The important thing to remember is that everybody goes through these feelings; they just have different ways of showing it. The best thing to do when adjusting to a new place is to get involved with your school and neighbourhood as much as possible. It would be great if you can make a friend who can explain some of the new things about New Zealand to you. Most people in a new country like to do this. They are like cultural translators.

Good luck with your new adventure!"

Indeed, we have successfully navigated the five stages of culture shock – euphoria, negative criticism of the new culture, wanting to return home, resignation and finally acceptance.

For us, it has taken six years to finally feel comfortable with our new surroundings. Costa Rica is now "home!" We really feel that being here has added good years to our lives. We hope the information in this book will help you avoid making some of the mistakes we made.

ppendices

Appendix 1

Cost of Martin's Surgery in Costa Rica (US DOLLARS)
(Based on 1993 prices – they have increased a bit since
then)

Martin stayed in the hospital a total of 20 days.

SURGICAL TEAM - 8 DOCTORS	$6,000.
Primary surgeon	$3,000.
First assistant	1,000.
Second assistant	500.
Anaesthesiologists	1,000.
Hemoperfusionist	500.
Pre-op & post-op care (5 doctors)	7,436.
TOTAL DOCTOR'S FEES	$13,436.
HOSPITAL FEES	$ 6,000.

Included room charges (20 days), X-rays, operating room,
treatments, ECG, recuperation, oxymeter, aspirator, car-
diac monitor, ambulance, echocardiogram, X-ray technical,
laboratory, medical material, pharmaceutical, Holter studies.

TOTAL FEE - SURGERY & HOSPITAL   US$19,436.

In addition to the above fee, the air ambulance cost
$17,475.51 including doctor and nurse. Even though fees
for the year 2000 have undoubtedly increased, the cost
compared to the United States is still much less. I have
been told that a similar operation there could cost as
much as $100,000. Our insurance paid hotel expenses for

me to a maximum stay of 7 days. Be very sure to find out your insurance company's policy for pre-existing conditions and limitations.

Appendix 2
EXAMPLES OF COSTS FOR PLASTIC SURGERY (US DOLLARS)

Dr. Arnoldo Fournier, one of the foremost plastic surgeons here, says a three-night stay at the hospital is $1,000, and doctors' bills run between $1,800 and $3,000 for facial plastic surgery.

For liposuction and lipo sculpture, as well as breast enlargement and reduction, two nights at the hospital are needed ($400-$800) and doctors charge between $1,200 and $2,500.

Please note that these prices may have changed.

Appendix 3
COST OF HOUSEHOLD ITEMS IN COSTA RICA

Following is our shopping list to give you an idea of the cost of items in Costa Rica:

ITEM	1994	
	colones	US$
Ajax	176.50	1.13
Hair conditioner (33 oz)	759.50	4.90
Shampoo (33 oz)	759.50	4.90
Liquid wax (470 ml)	233.00	1.50
Green olives (280g)	334.00	2.15
Sponge with abrasive pad	60.05	.38
Tico cheese (200g)	198.50	1.28
Ragu spag. sauce (28oz)	681.00	4.39
Bran flakes (380g)	518.50	3.34
Plastic cutting board	1,134.50	7.31
Tortilla chips (175g)	120.50	.77
Spag. noodles (1,000g)	168.50	1.08
Smirnoff vodka (1,780ml)	2,149.00	13.86
Orange juice (1,900ml)	253.00	1.63
Mixed pickles (1,250g)	707.00	4.56
Pledge polish	314.00	2.02
Laundry soap (1,500g)	402.50	2.59
Cleaning soap (3,785g)	376.00	2.42
2 green peppers	80.00	.51
Green beans	60.00	.38
Can of tuna (184g)	128.00	.82
Can of mushrooms (425 ml)	391.00	2.52
Can tomato paste (170g)	52.50	.33
Can tomatoes (780g)	285.00	1.83
Sardines (124 g)	152.50	.98

The June 1994 colon/dollar exchange rate was 155=$1US. The October 1996 rate is 214=$1US. The October 2000 rate is 313=$1US, February 2001 is 320 = $1US.

(N.B. Even though the above prices are 1994 prices, the dollar value in 2000 is still the same because of the devaluation of the colon. The cost of groceries has not really increased for people living on US dollars. We can still buy a month's supply for our business for $300-$400.)